CARDIGANS

Sixth&Spring Books
233 Spring Street,
New York, NY 10013

Managing Editor
WENDY WILLIAMS

Senior Editor
MICHELLE BREDESON

Art Director
DIANE LAMPHRON

Design Layout and Photography
STEPHEN JESSUP

Vice President, Publisher
TRISHA MALCOLM

Creative Director
JOE VIOR

Production Manager
DAVID JOINNIDES

President
ART JOINNIDES

Library of Congress Control Number: 2009928027

ISBN: 978-1-933027-88-3

Manufactured in China

1 3 5 7 9 10 8 6 4 2

First Edition

CARDIGANS

Louisa Harding

Contents

INTRODUCTION

Being a girl who is actually never without a cardigan, of course I was excited by the idea of a cardigan book.

While imagining this book, I started to think about how much I love the humble cardigan. My cardigan love affair started as a teenager. I remember taking one of my grandmother's cast-offs—a black, machine-knitted number made from "courtelle." I made that cardigan my own by customizing it with vintage jet buttons. I loved that humble cardigan and wore it constantly, dressing it up and down depending on my mood—with only a bra underneath to make it sexy and with a man's shirt and belt to punk it up. I wore and wore it until it started to fall to pieces, and instead of wearing it out I wore it at home as my special "comfy cardi" when relaxing or feeling poorly. Today the hand-knitted cardigan bears little resemblance to my grandmother's dictionary interpretation: "a long-sleeved knitted jacket that fastens up the front". Today the humble cardigan can take on many different looks, and in this book I have explored many interpretations of that same "knitted jacket that fastens up the front". To me the image that springs to mind of the traditional cardigan is not a flattering picture, usually the cardigan is tightly fitted and knitted: very often in cream or another mundane color, with large cabled patterning; there are lots of buttons down the front, which are then securely fastened over an ample bosom and not worn by anyone under the age of 80. Not a flattering image or look for most women. As a curvy cardigan-wearing woman myself, I have come to realize that the cardigan needs to be a "freer" garment, one that will disguise our female flaws and enhance our charming assets.

In this book you will find very few traditional button-up-the-front cardigans."I have split the book into four chapters. Classics centers around patterns for the "classic" cardigan shapes (V-neck, crew neck, and collared), but all the patterns have a small twist—three-quarter-length sleeves to showcase that beautiful bracelet, flattering one-button fastenings, darted waist-shaping to enhance the female curve. All are simple and straightforward garments that would be useful additions to any wardrobe. The next chapter, Edgings, showcases cardigans that have interesting edging details, some knitted at the same time as the garment and some knitted in contrasting or complementary yarn and stitched on. All are simple to make but the finished result looks elegant and sophisticated. Lace, Cables, Fair Isle—this chapter features cardigans with added surface patterning—lace, cables, or Fair Isle. The final chapter, Dressing Up, takes the sweater out on the town and shows that the cardigan is indeed the ideal garment when dressing up, whether for a party, special occasion, or just to spice up your favorite jeans and T-shirt combination. Here we set about to dispel the myth of the cardigan as solely the work-a-day staple, bringing it into the light for a fresh, new turn.

The designs in this book have been taken from my yarn magazine collections. Each season I design my collections around an inspiration point, a central theme, which helps me pinpoint the yarns I want to use and the color palette I want to create. Since the patterns were first published some of the yarns and shades have become discontinued and availability may be limited, please refer to page 160 for more information regarding the interchangeability of yarns from the ever evolving range of Louisa Harding Yarns.'

You will find at the beginning of each pattern I explain the inspiration behind the design, the collection it has come from and the reason I wanted to include it in this compilation of cardigan patterns.

Please have fun with the patterns! In some instances we have re-photographed the design using a totally different yarn to show how just a simple yarn change can totally alter the garment's look. Do try to think outside of your preconceptions of this "knitted jacket that fastens up the front". In the patterns I have shown distinctive fastening interpretations, button placements, or brooches in favor of buttons. Add femininity to your garment by adding ribbons to the neck or waist and tying them into a lovely flattering bow, or fasten only the buttons at the waist, enhancing your ladylike charms.

I hope you enjoy this book and make the "humble" cardigan your friend. I think they are versatile, sexy and fun, and I truly am never without one.

Classic

The patterns here are all great examples of "classic" cardigan shapes. You will find patterns for V-neck, crew-neck and collared cardigans, however, all the patterns have a small twist—three-quarter length sleeves to ensure you showcase that beautiful bracelet, flattering one-button fastenings, darted waist shaping. This chapter has simple and straightforward garments—all of them essential additions to any wardrobe. Classic does not have to be staid, so choose a beautiful or interesting yarn to knit your cardigan in. Several of the patterns here exemplify how a change of yarn can completely transform the look of your garment. When you start with a classic and well-designed cardigan, you can make it your own by your yarn choice and how you customize it by adding a brooch or a belt. Classic can be contemporary and sexy.

MARGUERITE

Taken from my first yarn collection book, Gathering Roses, this gently fitted cardigan is a classic that flatters. I have used a beautiful variegated green shade of Impression to knit the garment and simply added a few knitted flowers to the cuffs. I love cardigans with three-quarter-length sleeves; they are not only practical but also a great way to showcase lovely jewelry.

TO FIT DRESS SIZE:

8	10	12	14	16	18	**US**
10	12	14	16	18	20	**UK**
38	40	42	44	46	48	**EU**

ACTUAL SIZE: Ease allowance approx 5 cm (2 in)

86	91	97	102	107	111	cm
34	36	38	40	42	43 ¾	in

FINISHED LENGTH:

56	56	58	58	60	60	cm
22	22	23	23	23 ½	23 ½	in

SLEEVE LENGTH:

36	36	37	37	38	38	cm
14 ¼	14 ¼	14 ½	14 ½	15	15	in

YARN
Knitted in double knitting–weight yarn.
2nd size photographed in Louisa Harding Impression sh. 4 Green

7	7	8	8	9	9	x 50g balls

Contrast shade for flowers (optional)
1 x 50g ball Impression sh. 2 Pink

NEEDLES
Pair of 3.25 mm (US 3) knitting needles
Pair of 4 mm (US 6) knitting needles

BUTTONS
9 small pearl buttons

TENSION/GAUGE
22 sts x 30 rows to 10 cm (4 in) square measured over st st using 4 mm (US 6) knitting needles.

BACK

Using 3.25 mm (US 3) needles cast on 194(210, 218, 234, 242, 250) sts.
Beg with a K row work 2 rows in st st.
Next row (RS) (dec): K1, (K2tog) to last st, K1.
(98(106, 110, 118, 122, 126)sts)
Next row: Purl.
Rib row 1: (K2, P2) 24(26, 27, 29, 30, 31) times, K2.
Rib row 2: (P2, K2) 24(26, 27, 29, 30, 31) times, P2.
These 2 rows form rib.
Work in rib for a further 8 rows, dec 0(1, 0, 1, 0, 0) sts at each end of last row, and ending with RS facing for next row. (98(104, 110, 116, 122, 126)sts)
Change to 4 mm (US 6) needles.
Next row (RS) (dec): K3, K2tog, K to last 5 sts, K2tog tbl, K3.
Working all decs as set by last row, cont in st st, dec 1 st at each end of every foll 6th row until there are 84(90, 96, 102, 108, 112) sts.
Cont to work without further shaping until work measures 25(25, 26, 26, 27, 27) cm **(10(10, 10¼, 10¼, 10½, 10½) in)**, ending with RS facing for next row.
Next row (RS) (inc): K3, M1, K to last 3 sts, M1, K3.
Working all incs as set by last row, cont in st st, inc 1 st at each end of every foll 6th row until there are 94(100, 106, 112, 118, 122) sts.
Cont to work without further shaping until work measures 38(38, 39, 39, 40, 40) cm **(15(15, 15¼, 15¼, 15¾, 15¾) in)**, ending with RS facing for next row.

SHAPE ARMHOLES

Cast off 4(5, 5, 6, 6, 6) sts at beg next 2 rows, and 3(3, 3, 4, 4, 4) sts at beg foll 2 rows. (80(84, 90, 92, 98, 102) sts)
Next row (RS) (dec): K3, K2tog, K to last 5 sts, K2tog tbl, K3.
Next row (WS) (dec): P3, P2tog tbl, P to last 5 sts, P2tog, P3.
Next row (RS) (dec): K3, K2tog, K to last 5 sts, K2tog tbl, K3.
Working all decs as set by last row, dec 1 st at each end of every foll alt row until 72(74, 76, 78, 82, 86) sts rem.
Cont without further shaping until armhole measures 18(18, 19, 19, 20, 20) cm **(7(7, 7½, 7½, 8, 8) in)**, ending with RS facing for next row.

SHAPE SHOULDERS AND BACK NECK

Cast off 7(7, 7, 8, 8, 9) sts at beg next 2 rows.
Cast off 7(7, 7, 8, 8, 9) sts, K until there are 9(10, 11, 10, 12, 12) sts on RH needle and turn, leaving rem sts on a holder.
Work both sides of neck separately.
Cast off 3 sts, P to end.
Cast off rem 6(7, 8, 7, 9, 9) sts.
With RS facing rejoin yarn to sts from holder, cast off center 26 sts, K to end.
Complete to match first side, reversing shapings and working an extra row before beg of shoulder shaping.

LEFT FRONT

Using 3.25 mm (US 3) needles cast on 98(106, 114, 114, 122, 130) sts.
Beg with a K row work 2 rows in st st.
Next row (RS) (dec): K1, (K2tog) to last st, K1.
(50(54, 58, 58, 62, 66) sts)
Next row: Purl.
Rib row 1: (K2, P2) 12(13, 14, 14, 15, 16) times, K2.
Rib row 2: (P2, K2) 12(13, 14, 14, 15, 16) times, P2.
These 2 rows form rib.
Work in rib for a further 8 rows, –(dec, dec, inc, -, dec) –(1, 2, 1, -, 2) sts across last row, and ending with RS facing for next row. (50(53, 56, 59, 62, 64) sts)
Change to 4 mm (US 6) needles.
Next row (RS) (dec): K3, K2tog, K to end.
Working all side decs as set by last row, cont in st st, dec 1 st at side edge of every foll 6th row until there are 43(46, 49, 52, 55, 57) sts.
Cont to work without further shaping until work measures 25(25, 26, 26, 27, 27) cm **(10(10, 10¼, 10¼, 10½, 10½) in)**, ending with RS facing for next row.
Next row (RS) (inc): K3, M1, K to end.
Working all side incs as set by last row, cont in st st, inc 1 st at side edge of every foll 6th row until there are 48(51, 54, 57, 60, 62) sts.
Cont to work without further shaping until work measures 38(38, 39, 39, 40, 40) cm **(15(15, 15¼, 15¼, 15¾, 15¾) in)**, ending with RS facing for next row.

SHAPE ARMHOLE AND FRONT NECK

Cast off 4(5, 5, 6, 6, 6) sts, K to last 5 sts, K2tog tbl, K3.
Work 1 row.
Cast off 3(3, 3, 4, 4, 4) sts, K to last 5 sts, K2tog tbl, K3.
(39(41, 44, 45, 48, 50) sts)
Work 1 row.
Next row (RS) (dec): K3, K2tog, K to last 5 sts, K2tog tbl, K3.
Next row (WS) (dec): P to last 5 sts, P2tog, P3.
Next row (RS) (dec): K3, K2tog, K to last 5 sts, K2tog tbl, K3.
Working all decs as set by last row, dec 1 st at each end of every foll alt row until 32(32, 31, 32, 33, 35) sts rem.
1st, 2nd, 3rd & 4th sizes only cont to dec as set at front neck edge only on every alt row until 28(29, 30, 31) sts rem.
Work 3 rows.
Next row (dec): K to last 5 sts, K2tog tbl, K3.
Working all neck decs as set by last row, cont in st st, dec 1 st at neck edge of every foll 4th row until there are 20(21, 22, 23, 25, 27) sts.
Cont without further shaping until armhole measures 18(18, 19, 19, 20, 20) cm **(7(7, 7½, 7½, 8, 8) in)**, ending with RS facing for next row.

SHAPE SHOULDERS AND BACK NECK

Cast off 7(7, 7, 8, 8, 9) sts at beg next row and foll alt row.
Work 1 row.
Cast off rem 6(7, 8, 7, 9, 9) sts.

Right front

Using 3.25 mm (US 3) needles cast on 98(106, 114, 114, 122, 130) sts.
Beg with a K row work 2 rows in st st.
Next row (RS) (dec): K1, (K2tog) to last st, K1.
(50(54, 58, 58, 62, 66) sts)
Next row: Purl.
Rib row 1: (K2, P2) 12(13, 14, 14, 15, 16) times, K2.
Rib row 2: (P2, K2) 12(13, 14, 14, 15, 16) times, P2.
These 2 rows form rib.
Work in rib for a further 8 rows, –(dec, dec, inc, -, dec) –(1, 2, 1, -, 2) sts across last row, and ending with RS facing for next row. (50(53, 56, 59, 62, 64) sts)
Change to 4 mm (US 6) needles.
Next row (RS) (dec): K to last 5 sts, K2tog tbl, K3.
Working all decs as set by last row, complete to match left front, reversing shapings and working an extra row before beg armhole, neck and shoulder shaping.

Sleeves (work both the same)

Using 3.25 mm (US 3) needles cast on 114(114, 118, 118, 122, 122) sts.
Beg with a K row work 2 rows in st st.
Next row (RS) (dec): K1, (K2tog) to last st, K1.
(58(58, 60, 60, 62, 62) sts)
Next row: Purl.
Rib row 1: P0(0, 1, 1, 2, 2), (K2, P2) 14 times, K2, P0(0, 1, 1, 2, 2).
Rib row 2: K0(0, 1, 1, 2, 2), (P2, K2) 14 times, P2, K0(0, 1, 1, 2, 2).
These 2 rows form rib.
Work in rib for a further 8 rows.
Change to 4 mm (US 6) needles.
Next row (RS) (inc): K3, M1, K to last 3 sts, M1, K3.
Working all incs as set by last row, cont in st st, inc 1 st at each end of every foll 10th row until there are 72(72, 76, 76, 80, 80) sts.
Work without further shaping until work measures 36(36, 38, 38, 40, 40) cm **(14¼(14¼, 15, 15, 15¾, 15¾) in)** from start, ending with RS facing for next row.

Shape sleevehead
Cast off 5 sts at beg next 2 rows and 3 sts at beg foll 2 rows. (56(56, 60, 60, 64, 64) sts)
Dec 1 st at each end of next 3 rows and 3 foll alt rows. (44(44, 48, 48, 52, 52) sts)
Work 3 rows.
Dec 1 st at each end of next row and 3 foll 4th rows. (36(36, 40, 40, 44, 44) sts)
Work 1 row.
Dec 1 st at each end of next row and 2 foll alt rows, then on every foll row to (24(24, 28, 28, 32, 32) sts.
Cast off 3 sts at beg next 4 rows. (12(12, 16, 16, 20, 20) sts)
Cast off rem sts.

Making up

Press/block as described in finishing techniques (pg 158). Join both shoulder seams using back stitch.

Buttonhole band
With RS facing and starting at cast-on edge of right front and using 3.25 mm (US 3) needles pick up and K86(86, 88, 88, 90, 90) sts to start of front neck shaping, K42(42, 44, 44, 46, 46) sts to shoulder and 17 sts to center back neck. (145(145, 149, 149, 153, 153) sts)
Next row (WS) (buttonholes): K60(60, 62, 62, 64, 64), (yo, K2tog, K7) 8 times, yo, K2tog, K to end.
Next row (RS): Knit.
Cast off Kwise on **WS**.

Buttonband
With RS facing and starting at center back neck, and using 3.25 mm (US 3) needles pick up and K17 sts to shoulder, 42(42, 44, 44, 46, 46) sts down left front to start of front neck shaping and 86(86, 88, 88, 90, 90) sts to cast-on edge. (145(145, 149, 149, 153, 153) sts)
Knit 2 rows.
Cast off Kwise on **WS**.
Join edging at back neck.
Join side and sleeve seams.
Place center of cast-off edge of sleeve to shoulder seam. Set in sleeve, easing sleevehead into armhole.
Sew on buttons to correspond with buttonholes.

Flowers (make 10) (optional)
Using 4 mm (US 6) knitting needles and contrast yarn cast on 36 sts.
Row 1: K1, cast off 4 (2 sts on needle),*K1, cast off 4, rep from * to end. (12 sts on needle)
Break yarn and thread through rem sts, pull tight. Stitch flowers into place randomly on sleeves.

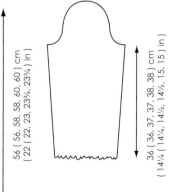

56 (56, 58, 58, 60, 60) cm
(22 (22, 23, 23¾, 23¾) in)

36 (36, 37, 37, 38, 38) cm
(14¼ (14¼, 14½, 14½, 15, 15) in)

43 (45.5, 48.5, 51, 53.5, 55.5) cm
(17 (18, 19, 20, 21, 22) in)

WILLOW

I adore this belted cardigan, taken from my Gathering Roses collection. I love the simplicity of this design. The belt is actually knitted at the same time as the back, which means that it can never get lost. The simple waist shaping ensures that there is no extra bulkiness around the middle. The rose embroidery is easy to do and completes the romantic feel of this garment.

TO FIT DRESS SIZE:

8-10	12	14	16-18	**US**
10-12	14	16	18-20	**UK**
38-40	42	44	46-48	**EU**

ACTUAL SIZE: Ease allowance approx 5-10 cm (2-4 in)

98	102	107	111	cm
38½	40	42	44	in

FINISHED LENGTH:

65	65	67	67	cm
25½	25½	26½	26½	in

SLEEVE LENGTH:

46	46	47	47	cm
18	18	18½	18½	in

YARN
Knitted in aran–weight yarn
1st size photographed in Louisa Harding Kashmir Aran sh. 6 Lime

15	16	17	17	x 50g balls

Contrast shade for embroidery
1 x 50g ball Louisa Harding Kimono Ribbon sh. 5 Forties

NEEDLES
Pair of 4.5 mm (US 7) knitting needles
Pair of 5 mm (US 8) knitting needles

TENSION/GAUGE
18 sts x 24 rows to 10 cm (4 in) square measured over st st using 5 mm (US 8) knitting needles.

BUTTONS
4 medium pearl buttons

Back

Using 4.5 (US 7) mm needles cast on 92(96, 100, 104) sts.
Knit 4 rows, ending with RS facing for next row.
Change to 5 mm (US 8) needles.
Knit 18 rows, ending with RS facing for next row.
Next row (RS) (dec): K3, K2togtbl, K to last 5 sts, K2tog, K3.
Working all decs as set by last row, cont in st st, dec 1 st at each end of every foll 6th row until there are 74(78, 82, 86) sts.
Cont to work without further shaping until work measures 26 cm **(10¼ in)**, ending with **WS** facing for next row.
Work jacket back and belt ties as folls:
Next row (WS) (inc): Purl, turn, and cast on 80 sts. (154(158, 162, 166) sts)
Next row (RS) (inc): Knit, turn, and cast on 80 sts. (234(238, 242, 246) sts)
Knit 17 rows, ending with RS facing for next row.
Next row (RS) (dec): Cast off 80 sts, knit to end. (154(158, 162, 166) sts)
Next row (WS) (dec): Cast off 80 sts, purl to end. (74(78, 82, 86) sts)
Next row (RS) (inc): K3, M1, K to last 3 sts, M1, K3. (76(80, 84, 88) sts)
Working all incs as set by last row, cont in st st, inc 1 st at each end of every foll 6th row until there are 88(92, 96, 100) sts.
Cont to work without further shaping until work measures 47(47, 48, 48) cm **(18½(18½, 19, 19) in)**, ending with RS facing for next row.

Shape armholes

Cast off 5 sts at beg next 2 rows, and 3 sts at beg foll 2 rows. (72(76, 80, 84) sts)
Next row (RS) (dec): K3, K2tog tbl, K to last 5 sts, K2tog, K3.
Next row (WS) (dec): P3, P2tog, P to last 5 sts, P2tog tbl, P3.
Next row (RS) (dec): K3, K2tog tbl, K to last 5 sts, K2tog, K3.
Working all decs as set by last row, dec 1 st at each end of every foll alt row until 62(64, 68, 72) sts rem.
Cont without further shaping until armhole measures 18(18, 19, 19) cm **(7(7, 7½, 7½) in)**, ending with RS facing for next row.

Shape shoulders and back neck

Cast off 6(6, 7, 7) sts at beg next 2 rows.
Cast off 6(6, 7, 7) sts, K until there are 8(9, 9, 11) on RH needle and turn, leaving rem sts on a holder.
Work both sides of neck separately.
Cast off 3 sts, P to end.
Cast off rem 5(6, 6, 8) sts.
With RS facing rejoin yarn to sts from holder, cast off center 22 sts, K to end.
Complete to match first side, reversing shapings.

Pocket linings (work 2)

Using 5 mm (US 8) needles cast on 22 sts.
Work 30 rows in st st, ending with a WS row, leave sts on a holder.

Left front

Using 4.5 (US 7) mm needles cast on 46(48, 50, 52) sts.
Knit 4 rows, ending with RS facing for next row.
Change to 5 mm (US 8) needles.
Knit 18 rows, ending with RS facing for next row.
Next row (RS)(dec): K3, K2togtbl, K to end.
Working all decs as set by last row, cont in st st, dec 1 st at side edge of every foll 6th row until there are 41(43, 45, 47) sts, ending with RS facing for next row.

Place pocket

Next row: K3, K2tog tbl, K6, slip next 22 sts onto a holder, K across 22 sts from holder for first pocket lining, K to end.
Work 5 rows.
Cont to dec at side edge as set on next row and every foll 6th row until 37(39, 41, 43) sts rem.
Cont to work without further shaping until work measures 31 cm **(12¼ in)**, ending with RS facing for next row.
Next row (RS) (inc): K3, M1, K to end. (38(40, 42, 44) sts)
Working all incs as set by last row, cont in st st, inc 1 st at side edge of every foll 6th row until there are 44(46, 48, 50) sts.
Cont to work without further shaping until work measures 47(47, 48, 48) cm **(18½(18½, 19, 19) in)**, ending with RS facing for next row.

Shape armhole and front neck

Next row (RS) (dec): Cast off 5 sts, K to last 5 sts, K2tog, K3. (38(40, 42, 44) sts.
Work 1 row.
Next row (RS) (dec): Cast off 3 sts, K to last 5 sts, K2tog, K3. (34(36, 38, 40) sts)
Work 1 row.
Next row (RS) (dec): K3, K2tog tbl, K to last 5 sts, K2tog, K3.
Next row (WS) (dec): P to last 5 sts, P2tog tbl, P3.
Next row (RS) (dec): K3, K2tog tbl, K to last 5 sts, K2tog, K3.
Working all decs as set by last row, dec 1 st at each end of every foll alt row until 25(25, 27, 29) sts rem.
Work 3 rows.
Next row (dec): K to last 5 sts, K2tog, K3.
Working all neck decs as set by last row, cont in st st, dec 1 st at neck edge of every foll 4th row until there are 17(18, 20, 22) sts.
Cont without further shaping until armhole measures 18(18, 19, 19) cm **(7(7, 7½, 7½) in)**, ending with RS facing for next row.

Shape shoulder

Cast off 6(6, 7, 7) sts at beg next row and foll alt row.
Work 1 row.
Cast off rem 5(6, 6, 8) sts.

Right front

Using 4.5 (US 7) mm needles cast on 46(48, 50, 52) sts.
Knit 4 rows, ending with RS facing for next row.
Change to 5 mm (US 8) needles.
Knit 18 rows, ending with RS facing for next row.
Next row (RS) (dec): K to last 5 sts, K2tog, K3.
Working all decs as set by last row, cont in st st, dec 1 st at side edge of every foll 6th row until there are 41(43, 45, 47) sts, ending with RS facing for next row.

Place pocket

Next row: K8(10, 12, 14), slip next 22 sts onto a holder, K across 22 sts from holder for second pocket lining, K to last 5 sts, K2tog, K3.
Complete to match left front, reversing shapings, and working an extra row before beg armhole, neck and shoulder shaping.

Sleeves (work both the same)

Using 4.5 (US 7) mm needles cast on 50(50, 54, 54) sts.
Knit 4 rows, ending with RS facing for next row.
Change to 5 mm (US 8) needles.
Knit 32 rows, ending with RS facing for next row.
Next row (RS) (inc): K3, M1, K to last 3 sts, M1, K3.
Working all incs as set by last row, cont in st st, inc 1 st at each end of every foll 14th row until there are 60(60, 64, 64) sts.
Cont to work without further shaping until sleeve measures 46(46, 47, 47) cm **(18(18, 18½, 18½)in)**, ending with RS facing for next row.

Shape sleevehead

Cast off 4 sts at beg next 2 rows, and 3 sts at beg foll 2 rows. (46(46, 50, 50) sts)
Dec 1 st at each end of next 3 rows and 2 foll alt rows. (36(36, 40, 40) sts)
Work 3 rows.
Dec 1 st at each end of next row and 2 foll 4th rows. (30(30, 34, 34) sts)
Work 1 row.
Dec 1 st at each end of next row, then on 2 foll alt rows, then on foll row. (22(22, 26, 26) sts)
Cast off 3 sts at beg next 4 rows. (10(10, 14, 14) sts)
Cast off rem sts.

Making up

Press/block as described in finishing techniques (pg 158).
Join both shoulder seams using back stitch.

Buttonhole band

With RS facing and starting at cast-on edge of right front and using 4.5 mm (US 7) needles pick up and knit 94(94, 98, 98) sts to start of front neck shaping, 36(36, 38, 38) sts to shoulder, then 15 sts to center back neck. (145(145, 151, 151) sts)
Next row (WS) (buttonholes): K53(53, 55, 55), (yo, k2tog, K18) 3 times, yo, K2tog, K to end.
Next row (RS): Knit.
Cast off Kwise on **WS**.

Buttonband

With RS facing and starting at center back neck, pick up and knit 15 sts to shoulder, 36(36, 38, 38) sts down left front to start of front neck shaping, then 94(94, 98, 98) sts to cast-on edge. (145(145, 151, 151) sts)
Work 2 rows in garter st.
Cast off Kwise on **WS**.
Join edging at back neck.

Pocket tops (work both the same)

Using 4.5 mm (US 7) needles knit across 22 sts left on holder for pocket top.
Work 2 rows in garter st.
Cast off Kwise on **WS**.
Join side and sleeve seams.
Place center of cast-off edge of sleeve to shoulder seam. Set in sleeve, easing sleevehead into armhole.
Sew on buttons to correspond with buttonholes.

Embroidery

Photocopy template in book, enlarging rose motif to the desired size.
Trace this motif on to tissue paper, using the photograph as a guide, then pin the tissue paper on to right side of jacket front. Using contrast yarn, embroider rose motif onto front of jacket using back stitch. ～

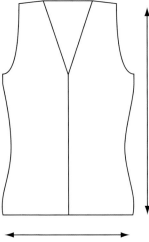
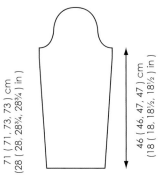

71 (71, 73, 73) cm
(28 (28, 28¾, 28¾) in

46 (46, 47, 47) cm
(18 (18, 18½, 18½) in)

49 (51, 53.5, 55.5) cm
(19¼ (20, 21, 22) in)

EMBROIDERY
Photocopy, enlarging
rose motif template to
desired size.
Trace this motif onto
tissue paper, then pin
the tissue paper onto
right side of jacket front.
Using contrasting yarn,
embroider rose motif
to front of jacket using
back stitch.

SABRINA

This is the ultimate classic crew-neck cardigan. Knitted using a double knitting-weight yarn, this sweater is so simply styled, and you can easily customize it: embellish by adding embroidery to the fronts, change the yarn used for the edgings, or play with the width of the stripes—the variations are limitless. The garment takes on a prim air when buttoned up, but when worn with just one button fastened it becomes a great cover-up.

TO FIT DRESS SIZE:

8	10	12	14	16	18	**US**
10	12	14	16	18	20	**UK**
38	40	42	44	46	48	**EU**

ACTUAL SIZE: Ease allowance approx 5 cm (2 in)

86	90	97	103	106	110	cm
34	35½	38 ¼	40½	41¾	43¼	in

FINISHED LENGTH:

48.5	48.5	50	50	52	52	cm
19	19	19 ¾	19 ¾	20 ½	20 ½	in

SLEEVE LENGTH:

36	36	38	38	40	40	cm
14¼	14¼	15	15	15¾	15¾	in

YARN

Knitted in double knitting–weight yarn
Stripe Cardigan
1st size photographed in Louisa Harding Grace
A. sh. 8 Purple

5	5	6	6	6	7	x 50g balls

B. sh. 6 Ruby

5	5	6	6	6	7	x 50g balls

One-color Cardigan
1st size photographed in Louisa Harding Kimono Angora
Pure sh. 7 Iris

6	6	7	7	8	8	x 25g balls

NEEDLES

Pair of 3.25 mm (US 3) knitting needles
Pair of 4 mm (US 6) knitting needles

BUTTONS

7 small mother of pearl

TENSION/GAUGE

22 sts x 30 rows to 10cm (4 in) square measured over striped st st using 4 mm (US 6) knitting needles

Striped Cardigan

Back

Using 3.25 mm (US 3) needles and yarn A cast on 85(89, 97, 103, 107, 111) sts.
Next row (RS): (K1, P1) to last st, K1.
Next row: (K1, P1) to last st, K1.
These 2 rows form moss st.
Work 2 more rows in moss st.
Change to 4 mm (US 6) needles and yarn B and work 10 rows in striped st st setting 4 row patt as folls:
2 rows B.
2 rows A.
Inc 1 st at each end of next row and every foll 14th row to 95(99, 107, 113, 117, 121) sts.
Work without further shaping until work measures 30.5(30.5, 31, 31, 32, 32) cm **(12, 12, 12¼, 12¼, 12½, 12½)in)** from cast-on edge, ending with RS facing for next row.

Shape armholes

Cast off 4(5, 6, 6, 6, 6) sts at beg next 2 rows and 3(3, 4, 4, 4, 4) sts at beg 2 foll rows. (81(83, 87, 93, 97, 101) sts)
Dec 1 st at both ends of next 3 rows and 1(1, 2, 4, 4, 4) foll alt rows. (73(75, 77, 79, 83, 87) sts)
Work without further shaping until work measures 18(18, 19, 19, 20, 20) cm **(7, 7, 7½, 7½, 8, 8)in)** from armhole, ending with RS facing for next row.

Shape shoulders and back neck

Cast off 7(7, 7, 7, 8, 8) sts at beg next 2 rows.
Cast off 7(7, 7, 7, 8, 8) sts, K until 9(10, 10, 11, 10, 12) sts remain on needle, turn, leave rem sts on a holder.
Cast off 3 sts, P to end.
Cast off rem 6(7, 7, 8, 7, 9) sts.
Rejoin yarn to rem sts, cast off center 27(27, 29, 29, 31, 31) sts, K to end.
Complete to match first side, reversing shapings.

Left front

Using 3.25 mm (US 3) needles and yarn A cast on 43(45, 49, 52, 54, 56) sts.
Next row (RS): (K1, P1) to last 1(1, 1, 0, 0, 0) st, K1(1, 1, 0, 0, 0).
Next row: K1(1, 1, 0, 0, 0), (P1, K1) to end.
These 2 rows form moss st.
Work 2 more rows in moss st.
Change to 4 mm (US 6) needles and yarn B and work 10 rows in striped st st setting 4 row patt as folls:
2 rows B.
2 rows A.
Inc 1 st at beg next row and every foll 14th row to 48(50, 54, 57, 59, 61) sts.
Work without further shaping until work measures 30.5(30.5, 31, 31, 32, 32) cm **(12, 12, 12¼, 12¼, 12½, 12½)in)** from cast-on edge, ending with RS facing for next row.

Shape armhole

Cast off 4(5, 6, 6, 6, 6) sts at beg next row and 3(3, 4, 4, 4, 4) sts at beg foll alt row. (41(42, 44, 47, 49, 51) sts)
Work 1 row.
Dec 1 st at beg next 3 rows and 1(1, 2, 4, 4, 4) foll alt rows. (37(38, 39, 40, 42, 44) sts)
Work without further shaping until front is 11 rows shorter than back to shoulder, ending with **WS** facing for next row.

Shape neck

Cast off 10(10, 11, 11, 12, 12) sts at beg next row and 4 sts at beg foll alt row. (23(24, 24, 25, 26, 28) sts)
Dec 1 st at neck edge on next 3 rows. (20(21, 21, 22, 23, 25) sts)
Work until front matches back to shoulder, ending with RS facing for next row.

Shape shoulder

Cast off 7(7, 7, 7, 8, 8) sts at beg next row and foll alt row.
Work 1 row.
Cast off rem 6(7, 7, 8, 7, 9) sts.

Right front

Using 3 .25 mm (US 3) needles and yarn A cast on 43(45, 49, 52, 54, 56) sts.
Next row (RS): (K1, P1) to last 1(1, 1, 0, 0, 0) st, K1(1, 1, 0, 0, 0).
Next row: K1(1, 1, 0, 0, 0), (P1, K1) to end.
These 2 rows form moss st.
Work 2 more rows in moss st.
Change to 4 mm (US 6) needles and yarn B and work 10 rows in striped st st setting 4 row patt as folls:
2 rows B.
2 rows A.
Inc 1 st at end of next row and every foll 14th row to 48(50, 54, 57, 59, 61) sts.
Complete to match left front, reversing shapings and working an extra row before beg armhole, neck, and shoulder shaping.

Sleeves (work both the same)

Using 3.25 mm (US 3) needles and yarn A cast on 59(59, 61, 61, 63, 63) sts.
Next row (RS): (K1, P1) to last st, K1.
Next row: (K1, P1) to last st, K1.
These 2 rows form moss st.
Work 2 more rows in moss st.
Change to 4 mm (US 6) needles and yarn B and work 10 rows in striped st st setting 4 row patt as folls:
2 rows B.
2 rows A.
Inc 1 st at each end of next row and every foll 14th(14th, 12th, 12th, 12th, 12th) row to 71(71, 75, 75, 79, 79) sts.
Work without further shaping until work measures

36(36, 38, 38, 40, 40) cm **(14¼, 14¼, 15, 15, 15¾, 15¾)in)** from cast on-edge, ending with RS facing for next row.

Shape sleevehead
Cast off 5 sts at beg next 2 rows and 3 sts at beg 2 foll rows. (55(55, 59, 59, 63, 63) sts)
Dec 1 st at each end of next 3 rows and 2 foll alt rows. (45(45, 49, 49, 53, 53) sts)
Work 3 rows.
Dec 1 st at each end of next row and 4 foll 4th rows. (35(35, 39, 39, 43, 43) sts)
Work 1 row.
Dec 1 st at each end of next row and foll alt row, then every row until 25(25, 29, 29, 33, 33) sts rem, ending with RS facing for next row.
Cast off 3 sts at beg next 4 rows.
Cast off rem 13(13, 17, 17, 21, 21) sts.

Making up

Press/block as described in finishing techniques (pg 158).
Join both shoulder seams using back stitch.

Buttonhole band
With RS of right front facing and using 3.25 mm (US 3) needles and yarn A, pick up and K 97(97, 103, 103, 109, 109) sts up right front to neck.
Work in moss st as folls:
Next row (WS): (K1, P1) to last st, K1.
Next row (RS) (buttonholes): K1, *patt 2 tog, yo, patt 14(14, 15, 15, 16, 16), rep from * to end.
Next row (WS): (K1, P1) to last st, K1.
Cast off in moss st.

Buttonband
With RS of left front facing and using 3.25 mm (US 3) needles and yarn A, pick up and K97(97, 103, 103, 109, 109) sts down left front.
Work 3 rows in moss st.
Cast off in moss st.

Neck band
With RS facing of right front and using 3.25 mm (US 3) needles and yarn A, pick up and K 3 sts from front band, 23(23, 24, 24, 25, 25) sts up right front neck to shoulder, 33(33, 35, 35, 37, 37) sts across back neck and 23(23, 24, 24, 25, 25) sts down left front neck, and 3 sts from front band. (85(85, 89, 89, 93, 93) sts)
Next row (WS): (K1, P1) to last st, K1.
Next row (RS) (buttonhole): K1, P2 tog, yo, patt to end.
Next row (WS): (K1, P1) to last st, K1.
Cast off in moss st.
Join side and sleeve seams.
Place center of cast-off edge of sleeve to shoulder seam. Set in sleeve, easing sleevehead into armhole.
Sew on buttons to correspond with buttonholes.

One-Color Cardigan

Work as for striped cardigan working in one color throughout.

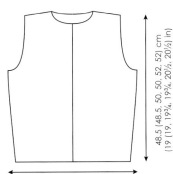
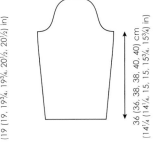

48.5 (48.5, 50, 50, 52, 52) cm
(19 (19, 19¾, 19¾, 20½, 20½) in)

43 (45, 48.5, 51.5, 53, 55) cm
(17 (17¾, 19, 20¼, 21, 21¾) in)

36 (36, 38, 38, 40, 40) cm
(14¼ (14¼, 15, 15, 15¾, 15¾) in)

GYPSY

This little Grecian-inspired bolero-style cardigan is a great classic piece. Originally I used a variegated ribbon yarn to knit the main body of the garment, making it ideal as a summer cover-up over a fluttery dress. Changing the yarn combination totally transforms the look—for example, using a sparkle yarn for the edging just lifts this garment out of the ordinary and makes it a great introduction to yarn combining. Alternatively this piece could be knitted in all one shade for a totally classical look.

TO FIT DRESS SIZE:

8	10	12	14	16	18	**US**
10	12	14	16	18	20	**UK**
38	40	42	44	46	48	**EU**

ACTUAL SIZE: Ease allowance approx 5 cm (2 in)

86	90	97	101	106	110	cm
34	35½	38¼	39¾	41¾	43¼	in

FINISHED LENGTH:

30.5	30.5	33	33	35.5	35.5	cm
12	12	13	13	14	14	in

SLEEVE LENGTH:

4	4	4	4	4	4	cm
1½	1½	1½	1½	1½	1½	in

YARN

Knitted in aran–weight yarn
1st size photographed in Louisa Harding Nautical Cotton and Kimono Ribbon
A. Nautical Cotton sh. 20 Butter

1	1	1	1	1	1	x 50g balls

B. Kimono Ribbon sh. 12 Abalone

4	4	4	5	5	5	x 50g balls

1st size photographed in Louisa Harding Glisten and Kashmir Aran
A. Glisten sh. 29 Bronze

1	1	1	1	1	1	x 50g balls

B. Kashmir Aran sh. 21 Strawberry

5	5	6	6	7	7	x 50g balls

NEEDLES

Kimono Ribbon garment
Pair of 4.5 mm (US 7) knitting needles
Pair of 6 mm (US 10) knitting needles
Kashmir Aran garment
Pair of 4.5 mm (US 7) knitting needles
Pair of 5 mm (US 8) knitting needles

BUTTONS

6 small mother of pearl

TENSION/GAUGE

18 sts x 24 rows to 10cm (4 in) square measured over st st using largest size knitting needles and yarn B

BACK

Using largest size needles and yarn A work picot cast-on as folls:
Cast on 5 sts using the cable cast-on method, cast off 2 sts, slip st on RH needle back onto LH needle (3 sts now on LH needle) rep from * to * until 69(75, 81, 84, 87, 93) sts on needle, cast on 2(0, 0, 1, 2, 0) sts.
(71(75, 81, 85, 89, 93) sts)
Change to smallest size needles and work 2 rows in garter st.
Change to yarn B and work 2 rows in garter st.
Change to largest size needles and beg with a K row work 4(4, 6, 6, 6, 6) rows in st st, ending with RS facing for next row.
Next row (RS) (inc): K3, M1, K to last 3 sts, M1, K3.
Work 5(5, 7, 7, 7, 7) rows.
Inc 1 st as above on next row and foll 6th(6th, 8th, 8th, 8th, 8th) row. (77(81, 87, 91, 95, 99) sts)
Cont to work without further shaping until work measures 12.5(12.5, 14, 14, 15.5, 15.5)cm **(5(5, 5½, 5½, 6, 6)in)** from cast-on edge, ending with RS facing for next row.

SHAPE ARMHOLES

Cast off 3(4, 6, 6, 7, 8) sts at beg next 2 rows and 3(3, 3, 4, 4, 4) sts at beg 2 foll rows. (65(67, 69, 71, 73, 75) sts)
Dec 1 st at each end of next row and 3 foll alt rows.
(57(59, 61, 63, 65, 67) sts)
Cont without further shaping until armhole measures 18(18, 19, 19, 20, 20)cm **(7(7, 7½, 7½, 8, 8)in)**, ending with RS facing for next row.

SHAPE SHOULDERS AND BACK NECK

Cast off 5(5, 5, 5, 5, 6) sts at beg next 2 rows.
Cast off 5(5, 5, 5, 5, 6) sts, K until there are 7(8, 8, 9, 9, 8) on RH needle and turn, leaving rem sts on a holder.
Work both sides of neck separately.
Cast off 3 sts, P to end.
Cast off rem 4(5, 5, 6, 6, 5) sts.
With RS facing rejoin yarn to sts from holder, cast off center 23(23, 25, 25, 27, 27) sts, K to end.
Complete to match first side, reversing shapings.

LEFT FRONT

Using largest size needles and yarn A work picot cast-on as folls:
Cast on 5 sts using the cable cast-on method, cast off 2 sts, slip st on RH needle back onto LH needle (3 sts now on LH needle) rep from * to * until 36(36, 39, 42, 45, 45) sts on needle, cast on 0(2, 2, 1, 0, 2) sts.
(36(38, 41, 43, 45, 47) sts)
Change to smallest size needles and work 2 rows in garter st.
Change to yarn B and work 2 rows in garter st.

Change to largest size needles and beg with a K row work 4(4, 6, 6, 6, 6) rows in st st, ending with RS facing for next row.
Next row (RS) (inc): K3, M1, K to end.
Work 5(5, 7, 7, 7, 7) rows.
Inc 1 st as above on next row and foll 6th(6th, 8th, 8th, 8th, 8th) row. (39(41, 44, 46, 48, 50) sts)
Cont to work without further shaping until work measures 12.5(12.5, 14, 14, 15.5, 15.5)cm **(5(5, 5½, 5½, 6, 6)in)** from cast-on edge, ending with RS facing for next row.

SHAPE ARMHOLE

Cast off 3(4, 6, 6, 7, 8) sts at beg next row and 3(3, 3, 4, 4, 4) sts at beg foll alt row. (33(34, 35, 36, 37, 38) sts)
Work 1 row.
Dec1 st at beg of next row and 3 foll alt rows.
(29(30, 31, 32, 33, 34) sts)
Cont without further shaping until front is 13 rows shorter than back to shoulder shaping, ending with **WS** facing for next row.

SHAPE NECK

Cast off 9(9, 10, 10, 11, 11) sts at beg next row.
Dec 1 st at neck edge on next 4 rows and 2 foll alt rows.
(14(15, 15, 16, 16, 17) sts)
Cont straight until left front matches back to start of shoulder shaping, ending with RS facing for next row.

SHAPE SHOULDER

Cast off 5(5, 5, 5, 5, 6) sts at beg next row and foll alt row.
Work 1 row.
Cast off rem 4(5, 5, 6, 6, 5) sts.

RIGHT FRONT

Using largest size needles and yarn A work picot cast-on as folls:
Cast on 5 sts using the cable cast-on method, cast off 2 sts, slip st on RH needle back onto LH needle (3 sts now on LH needle) rep from * to * until 36(36, 39, 42, 45, 45) sts on needle, cast on 0(2, 2, 1, 0, 2) sts.
(36(38, 41, 43, 45, 47) sts)
Change to smallest size needles and work 2 rows in garter st.
Change to yarn B and work 2 rows in garter st.
Change to largest size needles and beg with a K row work 4(4, 6, 6, 6, 6) rows in st st, ending with RS facing for next row.
Next row (RS) (inc): K to last 3 sts, M1, K3.
Work 5(5, 7, 7, 7, 7) rows.
Inc 1 st as above on next row and foll 6th(6th, 8th, 8th, 8th, 8th) row. (39(41, 44, 46, 48, 50) sts)
Complete to match left front, reversing shapings and working an extra row before beg armhole, neck and shoulder shaping.

SLEEVES (work both the same)

Using largest size needles and yarn A work picot cast-on as folls:
Cast on 5 sts using the cable cast-on method, cast off 2 sts, slip st on RH needle back onto LH needle (3 sts now on LH needle) rep from * to * until 51(51, 57, 57, 60, 60) sts on needle, cast on 2(2, 0, 0, 1, 1) sts.
(53(53, 57, 57, 61, 61) sts)
Change to smallest size needles and work 2 rows in garter st.
Change to yarn B and work 2 rows in garter st.
Change to largest size needles and beg with a K row work 6 rows in st st, ending with RS facing for next row.

SHAPE SLEEVEHEAD

Cast off 5(5, 6, 6, 7, 7) sts at beg next 2 rows.
(43(43, 45, 45, 47, 47) sts)
Dec 1 st at each end of next 3 rows and 2 foll alt rows.
(33(33, 35, 35, 37, 37) sts)
Work 3 rows.
Dec 1 st at each end of next row and 3 foll 4th rows.
(25(25, 27, 27, 29, 29) sts)
Work 1 row.
Dec 1 st at each end of next row and foll alt row, then at each end of foll row. (19(19, 21, 21, 23, 23) sts)
Cast off 3 sts at beg next 4 rows.
Cast off rem 7(7, 9, 9, 11, 11) sts.

MAKING UP

Press/block as described in finishing techniques (pg 158). Join both shoulder seams and side seams using back stitch.

BUTTONHOLE BAND

With RS of right front facing and using smallest needles and yarn A, pick up and K 40(40, 42, 42, 44, 44) sts up to right front to neck.
Next row (WS): Knit.
Next row (RS) (buttonholes): K2, (yo, k2tog, K6) 4 times, yo, k2tog, K4(4, 6, 6, 8, 8).
Cast off Kwise on **WS**.

BUTTONBAND

With RS of left front facing and using smallest size needles and yarn A, pick up K 40(40, 42, 42, 44, 44) sts down left front end.
Work 2 rows in garter st.
Cast off Kwise on **WS**.

NECK EDGING

With RS of right front facing and using smallest size needles and yarn A, pick up and K 2 sts from front band, 22(22, 23, 23, 24, 24) sts up right front neck to shoulder, 29(29, 31, 31, 33, 33) sts across back neck and 22(22, 23, 23, 24, 24) sts down left front, and 2 sts from front band.
(77(77, 81, 81, 85, 85) sts)
Next row (WS): Knit.
Next row (RS) (buttonhole): K2, yo, k2tog, K to end.
Cast off in Kwise (on WS).
Join side seams.
Place center of cast-off edge of sleeve to shoulder seam. Set in sleeve, easing sleevehead into armhole.
Sew on buttons to correspond with buttonholes.

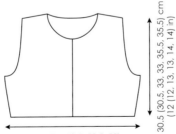

30.5 (30.5, 33, 33, 35.5, 35.5) cm
(12 (12, 13, 13, 14, 14) in)

42.5 (45, 48.5, 50.5, 52.5, 55) cm
(16¾ (17¾, 19, 20, 20¾, 21¾) in)

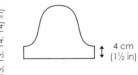

4 cm
(1½ in)

SYLPH

This simple V-neck cardigan is photographed in two completely contrasting yarns. The original was knitted using a nylon yarn with sequins running through it, which makes a beautifully bold statement. I wanted also to show how using a straight spun yarn such as the Mulberry Silk showcases the simplicity of this piece and how versatile this shape is for many body shapes. Try adding a belt to cinch in the waist and flatter the curves.

To fit dress size:

8	10	12	14	16	18	US
10	12	14	16	18	20	UK
38	40	42	44	46	48	EU

Actual size: Ease allowance approx 5 cm (2 in)

86	91	96	102	107	111	cm
34	36	37 ¾	40¼	42	43¾	in

Finished length:

48.5	48.5	51	51	53.5	53.5	cm
19	19	20	20	21	21	in

Sleeve length:

35.5	35.5	35.5	35.5	35.5	35.5	cm
14	14	14	14	14	14	in

Yarn
Knitted in double knitting–weight yarn
1st size photographed in Louisa Harding Coquette
sh. 4 Gold

12	12	13	14	15	15	x 25g balls

1st size photographed in Louisa Harding Mulberry Silk
sh. 10 Rust

7	7	7	8	8	9	x 50g balls

Needles
Pair of 3.25 mm (US 3) knitting needles
Pair of 4 mm (US 6) knitting needles

Buttons
6 small pearl buttons

Tension/gauge
22 sts x 30 rows to 10 cm (4 in) square measured over st st using 4 mm (US 6) knitting needles.

BACK

Using 3.25 mm (US 3) needles cast on 84(90, 96, 102, 108, 112) sts.
Beg with a K row work 4 rows in st st.
Change to 4 mm (US 6) needles and work 4 rows in garter st.
Beg with a K row work 10 rows in st st.
Next row (RS) (inc): K3, M1, K to last 3 sts, M1, K3.
(86(92, 98, 104, 110, 114) sts)
Beg with a P row work 9 rows in st st.
Inc as above on next row and 3 foll 10th rows.
(94(100, 106, 112, 118, 122) sts)
Cont to work without further shaping until work measures 30.5(30.5, 32, 32, 33.5, 33.5)cm **(12(12, 12¾, 12¾, 13¼, 13¼)in)**, ending with RS facing for next row.

SHAPE ARMHOLES

Cast off 4(6, 7, 9, 9, 9) sts at beg next 2 rows, and 3(3, 4, 4, 5, 5) sts at beg foll 2 rows. (80(82, 84, 86, 90, 94) sts)
Next row (RS) (dec): K3, K2tog, K to last 5 sts, K2tog tbl, K3.
Next row: Purl.
Dec as above on next row and 2 foll alt rows.
(72(74, 76, 78, 82, 86) sts)
Cont without further shaping until armhole measures 18(18, 19, 19, 20, 20)cm **(7(7, 7½, 7½, 8, 8)in)**, ending with RS facing for next row.

SHAPE SHOULDERS AND BACK NECK

Cast off 7(7, 7, 8, 8, 9) sts at beg next 2 rows.
Cast off 7(7, 7, 8, 8, 9) sts, K until there are 9(10, 11, 10, 12, 12) sts on RH needle and turn, leaving rem sts on a holder.
Work both sides of neck separately.
Cast off 3 sts, P to end.
Cast off rem 6(7, 8, 7, 9, 9) sts.
With RS facing rejoin yarn to sts from holder, cast off center 26 sts, K to end.
Complete to match first side, reversing shapings.

LEFT FRONT

Using 3.25 mm (US 3) needles cast on 42(45, 48, 51, 54, 56) sts.
Beg with a K row work 4 rows in st st.
Change to 4 mm (US 6) needles and work 4 rows in garter st.
Beg with a K row work 10 rows in st st.
Next row (RS) (inc): K3, M1, K to end.
(43(46, 49, 52, 55, 57) sts)
Beg with a P row work 9 rows in st st.
Inc as above on next row and 3 foll 10th rows.
(47(50, 53, 56, 59, 61) sts)
Cont to work without further shaping until work measures 30.5(30.5, 32, 32, 33.5, 33.5)cm **(12(12, 12¾, 12¾, 13¼, 13¼)in)**, ending with RS facing for next row.

SHAPE ARMHOLE

Cast off 4(6, 7, 9, 9, 9) sts at beg next row and 3(3, 4, 4, 5, 5) sts at beg foll alt row. (40(41, 42, 43, 45, 47) sts)
Work 1 row.

SHAPE ARMHOLE AND FRONT NECK

Next row (RS) (dec): K3, K2tog, K to last 5 sts, K2tog tbl, K3.
(38(39, 40, 41, 43, 45) sts)
Next row: Purl.
Dec as above on next row and 2 foll alt rows.
(32(33, 34, 35, 37, 39) sts)
Next row: Purl.
Dec as set at neck edge only on next row and 4 foll alt rows, then on every foll 4th row to 20(21, 22, 23, 25, 27) sts.
Cont without further shaping until armhole measures 18(18, 19, 19, 20, 20)cm **(7(7, 7½, 7½, 8, 8)in)**, ending with RS facing for next row.

SHAPE SHOULDER

Cast off 7(7, 7, 8, 8, 9) sts at beg next row and foll alt row.
Work 1 row.
Cast off rem 6(7, 8, 7, 9, 9) sts.

RIGHT FRONT

Using 3.25 mm (US 3) needles cast on 42(45, 48, 51, 54, 56) sts.
Beg with a K row work 4 rows in st st.
Change to 4 mm (US 6) needles and work 4 rows in garter st.
Beg with a K row work 10 rows in st st.
Next row (RS) (inc): K to last 3 sts, M1, K3.
(43(46, 49, 52, 55, 57) sts)
Beg with a P row work 9 rows in st st.
Inc as above on next row and 3 foll 10th rows.
(47(50, 53, 56, 59, 61) sts)
Complete to match left front, reversing shapings and working an extra row before beg armhole, neck, and shoulder shaping.

SLEEVES (work both the same)

Using 3.25 mm (US 3) needles cast on 56(56, 60, 60, 64, 64) sts.
Beg with a K row work 4 rows in st st.
Change to 4 mm (US 6) needles and work 4 rows in garter st.
Beg with a K row work 10 rows in st st.
Next row (RS) (inc): K3, M1, K to last 3 sts, M1, K3.
(58(58, 62, 62, 66, 66) sts)
Beg with a P row work 15 rows in st st.
Inc as above on next row and 3 foll 16th rows.
(66(66, 70, 70, 74, 74) sts)
Cont to work without further shaping until work measures 35cm **(14 in)**, ending with RS facing for next row.

Shape sleevehead

Cast off 5(5, 6, 6, 7, 7) sts at beg next 2 rows, and 3 sts at beg foll 2 rows. (50(50, 52, 52, 54, 54) sts)
Dec 1 st at each end of next 3 rows and 4 foll alt rows. (36(36, 38, 38, 40, 40) sts)
Work 3 rows.
Dec 1 st at each end of next row and 3 foll 4th rows. (28(28, 30, 30, 32, 32) sts)
Work 1 row.
Dec 1 st at each end of next row and 2 foll alt rows, dec 1 st at ech end of foll row. (20(20, 22, 22, 24, 24) sts).
Cast off 3 sts at beg next 4 rows.
Cast off rem 8(8, 10, 10, 12, 12) sts.

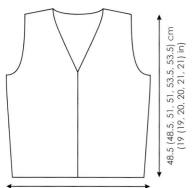
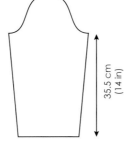

48.5 (48.5, 51, 51, 53.5, 53.5) cm
(19 (19, 20, 20, 21, 21) in)

35.5 cm
(14 in)

42.5 (45.5, 48, 51, 53.5, 55.5) cm
(16¾ (18, 19, 20, 21, 22) in)

Making up

Press/block as described in finishing techniques (pg 158).
Join both shoulder seams using back stitch.

Buttonhole band

With RS facing and starting at cast-on edge of right front and using 3.25 mm (US 3) needles pick up and K 68(68, 72, 72, 78, 78) sts to start of front neck shaping, K42(42, 44, 44, 46, 46) sts to shoulder and 17 sts to center back neck. (127(127, 133, 133, 141, 141) sts)
Next row (WS) (buttonholes): K59(59, 60, 60, 63, 63), [yo, K2tog, K11(11, 12, 12, 13, 13)] 5 times, yo, K2tog, K1.
Next row (RS): Knit.
Cast off Kwise on **WS**.

Buttonband

With RS facing and starting at center back neck, and using 3.25 mm (US 3) needles pick up and K 17 sts to shoulder, K42(42, 44, 44, 46, 46) sts down left front to start of front neck shaping and K68(68, 72, 72, 78, 78) sts to cast-on edge. (127(127, 133, 133, 141, 141) sts)
Knit 2 rows.
Cast off Kwise on **WS**.
Join edging at back neck.
Join side and sleeve seams.
Place center of cast-off edge of sleeve to shoulder seam. Set in sleeve, easing sleevehead into armhole.
Sew on buttons to correspond with buttonholes.

OTELLO

This simple little jacket is a classic go-anywhere piece. This design is taken from my collection Venezia, which we were lucky enough to photograph in Venice itself, rising very early in the morning to beat the crowds. This garment is photographed on the Rialto Bridge. I love the way the gray and white marble's coolness enhances the intensity of the blue yarn.

TO FIT DRESS SIZE:

8	10	12	14	16	18	US
10	12	14	16	18	20	UK
38	40	42	44	46	48	EU

ACTUAL SIZE: Ease allowance approx 10 cm (4 in)

91	97	103	107	112	118	cm
36	38	40½	42	44	46½	in

FINISHED LENGTH:

53.5	53.5	56	56	58.5	58.5	cm
21	21	22	22	23	23	in

SLEEVE LENGTH:

35.5	35.5	38	38	40.5	40.5	cm
14	14	15	15	16	16	in

YARN

Knitted in bulky-weight yarn
1st size photographed in Louisa Harding Ca'd'Oro
sh. 7 Midnight

10	11	12	12	13	14	x 50g balls

NEEDLES

Pair of 6 mm (US 10) knitting needles
Pair of 7 mm (US 10 ½) knitting needles

BUTTONS

6 large buttons

TENSION/GAUGE

13 sts x 17 rows to 10 cm (4 in) square measured over st st using 7 mm (US 10 ½) knitting needles.

Back

Using 6 mm (US 10) needles cast on 59(63, 67, 69, 73, 77) sts.
Work 20 rows in garter st, ending with RS facing for next row.
Change to 7 mm (US 10½) needles.
Beg with a K row work 4 rows in st st.
Next row (RS) (dec): K3, K2tog, K to last 5 sts, K2tog tbl, K3. (57(61, 65, 67, 71, 75) sts)
Work 3 rows.
Dec 1 st at each end internally as above on next row and 2 foll 4th rows. (51(55, 59, 61, 65, 69) sts)
Work without further shaping until work measures 24.5 cm (**9½ in**) ending with RS facing for next row.
Next row (RS) (inc): K3, M1, K to last 3 sts, M1, K3. (53(57, 61, 63, 67, 71) sts)
Work 3 rows.
Inc 1 st at each end internally as above on next row and 2 foll 4th rows. (59(63, 67, 69, 73, 77) sts)
Work without further shaping until work measures 33(33, 35, 35, 35.5, 35.5) cm (**13(13, 13½, 13½, 14, 14)in**) from cast-on edge, ending with RS facing for next row.

Shape armholes

Cast off 3(3, 3, 4, 4, 5) sts at beg next 2 rows and 3 sts beg 2 foll rows. (47(51, 55, 55, 59, 61) sts)
Dec 1 st at both ends of next row and 0(1, 2, 2, 3, 3) foll alt rows. (45(47, 49, 49, 51, 53) sts)
Work without further shaping until work measures 20.5(20.5, 22, 22, 23, 23) cm (**8(8, 8½, 8½, 9, 9)in**) from armhole, ending with RS facing for next row.

Shape shoulders and back neck

Cast off 4 sts beg next 2 rows.
Cast off 4 sts, K until there are 7(8, 8, 8, 8, 9) sts on RH needle and turn, leaving rem sts on a holder.
Work both sides of neck separately.
Cast off 3 sts, P to end.
Cast off rem 4(5, 5, 5, 5, 6) sts.
With RS rejoin yarn to rem sts, cast off 15(15, 17, 17, 19, 19) sts, K to end.
Complete to match first side, reversing shapings.

Left front

Using 6 mm (US 10) needles cast on 22(24, 26, 27, 29, 31) sts.
Edging row 1 (RS) (inc): K to last 3 sts, M1, K3.
(23(25, 27, 28, 30, 32) sts)
Edging row 2 (inc): K3, M1, K to end.
(24(26, 28, 29, 31, 33) sts)
Edging row 3 (inc): K to last 3 sts, M1, K3.
(25(27, 29, 30, 32, 34) sts)
Edging row 4 (inc): K3, M1, K to end.
(26(28, 30, 31, 33, 35) sts)
Edging row 5 (inc): K to last 3 sts, M1, K3.
(27(29, 31, 32, 34, 36) sts)
Edging row 6: Knit.

Edging row 7 (inc): K to last 3 sts, M1, K3.
(28(30, 32, 33, 35, 37) sts)
Edging row 8: Knit.
Edging row 9 (inc): K to last 3 sts, M1, K3.
(29(31, 33, 34, 36, 38) sts)
Work 3 rows in garter st.
Edging row 13 (inc): K to last 3 sts, M1, K3.
(30(32, 34, 35, 37, 39) sts)
Work 7 rows in garter st, ending with RS facing for next row.
Change to 7 mm (US 10½) needles.
Beg with a K row work 4 rows in st st.
Next row (RS) (dec): K3, K2tog, K to end.
(29(31, 33, 34, 36, 38) sts)
Work 3 rows.
Dec 1 st internally as above on next row and 2 foll 4th rows. (26(28, 30, 31, 33, 35) sts)
Work without further shaping until work measures 24.5 cm (**9½ in**) ending with RS facing for next row.
Next row (RS) (inc): K3, M1, K to end.
(27(29, 31, 32, 34, 36) sts)
Work 3 rows.
Inc 1 st internally as above on next row and 2 foll 4th rows. (30(32, 34, 35, 37, 39) sts)
Work without further shaping until work measures 33(33, 35, 35, 35.5, 35.5) cm (**13(13, 13½, 13½, 14, 14)in**) from cast-on edge, ending with RS facing for next row.

Shape armhole

Cast off 3(3, 3, 4, 4, 5) sts at beg next row and 3 sts beg foll alt row. (24(26, 28, 28, 30, 31) sts)
Work 1 row.
Dec 1 st at beg of next row and 0(1, 2, 2, 3, 3) foll alt rows. (23(24, 25, 25, 26, 27) sts)
Work without further shaping until front is 9 rows shorter than back to shoulder, ending with **WS** facing for next row.

Shape front neck

Cast off 5(5, 6, 6, 7, 7) sts, P to end.
(18(19, 19, 19, 19, 20) sts)
Work 1 row.
Cast off 3 sts beg next row, P to end.
(15(16, 16, 16, 16, 17) sts)
Dec 1 st at neck edge on next 3 rows.
(12(13, 13, 13, 13, 14) sts)
Work until front matches back to shoulder, ending with RS facing for next row.

Shape shoulder

Cast off 4 sts beg next row and foll alt row.
Work 1 row.
Cast off rem 4(5, 5, 5, 5, 6) sts.

Right front

Using 6 mm (US 10) needles cast on 22(24, 26, 27, 29, 31) sts.
Edging row 1 (RS) (inc): K3, M1, K to end.
(23(25, 27, 28, 30, 32) sts)

Edging row 2 (inc): K to last 3 sts, M1, K3.
(24(26, 28, 29, 31, 33) sts)
Edging row 3 (inc): K3, M1, K to end.
(25(27, 29, 30, 32, 34) sts)
Edging row 4 (inc): K to last 3 sts, M1, K3.
(26(28, 30, 31, 33, 35) sts)
Edging row 5 (inc): K3, M1, K to end.
(27(29, 31, 32, 34, 36) sts)
Edging row 6: Knit.
Edging row 7 (inc): K3, M1, K to end.
(28(30, 32, 33, 35, 37) sts)
Edging row 8: Knit.
Edging row 9 (inc): K3, M1, K to end.
(29(31, 33, 34, 36, 38) sts)
Work 3 rows in garter st.
Edging row 13 (inc): K3, M1, K to end.
(30(32, 34, 35, 37, 39) sts)
Work 7 rows in garter st.
Change to 7 mm (US 10½) needles.
Beg with a K row work 4 rows in st st.
Next row (RS) (dec): K to last 5 sts, K2tog tbl, K3.
(29(31, 33, 34, 36, 38) sts)
Work 3 rows.
Dec 1 st internally as above on next row and 2 foll 4th
rows. (26(28, 30, 31, 33, 35) sts)
Work without further shaping until work measures
24.5 cm **(9½ in)** ending with RS facing for next row.
Next row (RS) (inc): K to last 3 sts, M1, K3.
(27(29, 31, 32, 34, 36) sts)
Work 3 rows.
Inc 1 st internally as above on next row and 2 foll 4th rows.
(30(32, 34, 35, 37, 39) sts)
Complete to match left front, reversing shapings and
working an extra row before beg armhole, neck, and
shoulder shaping.

SLEEVES (work both the same)

Using 6 mm (US 10) needles cast on 37(37, 39, 39, 41, 41) sts.
Work 20 rows in garter st.
Change to 7 mm (US 10 ½) needles.
Beg with a K row work 4 rows in st st, ending with RS
facing for next row.
Next row (RS) (inc): K3, M1, K to last 3 sts, M1, K3.
(39(39, 41, 41, 43, 43) sts)
Work 9 rows.
Inc 1 st at each end internally as above on next row
and every foll 10th row to 43(43, 45, 45, 47, 47) sts.
Work without further shaping until sleeve measures
35.5(35.5, 38, 38, 40.5, 40.5) cm **(14(14, 15, 15, 16, 16)in)**
from cast on edge ending with RS facing for next row.

SHAPE SLEEVEHEAD

Cast off 3(3, 3, 3, 4, 4) sts at beg next 2 rows.
(37(37, 39, 39, 39, 39) sts)
Dec 1 st at each end of next 3 rows and 6 foll alt rows.
(19(19, 21, 21, 21, 21) sts)
Dec 1 st at each end of next row. (17, 17, 19, 19, 19, 19) sts)

Cast off 3 sts at beg next 4 rows. (5(5, 7, 7, 7, 7) sts)
Cast off.

MAKING UP

Press/block as described in finishing techniques (pg 158).
Join both shoulder seams using back stitch.

BUTTONHOLE BAND
With RS facing of right front and using 6 mm (US 10)
needles and starting top of garter st hem pick up and
K54(54, 59, 59, 64, 64) sts up right front to neck.
Work 3 rows in garter st.
Next row (RS) (buttonholes): K1, [K2tog yo, K8(8, 9, 9,
10, 10)] 5 times, yo, K2tog, K1.
Work 4 rows in garter st ending with WS facing for next row.
Cast off Kwise on **WS**.

BUTTONBAND
With RS facing of left front and using 6 mm (US 10)
needles pick up and K54(54, 59, 59, 64, 64) sts down left
front to top of garter st hem.
Work 8 rows in garter st.
Cast off Kwise on **WS**.

COLLAR
Using 6 mm (US 10) needles cast on 59(59, 63, 63, 67, 67) sts.
Work in garter st until work measures 5 cm **(2 in)** from
cast on ending with RS facing for next row.
Next row (RS) (dec): K3, K2tog, K to last 5 sts, K2tog tbl,
K3. (57(57, 61, 61, 65, 65) sts)
Next row: Knit.
Dec as above on next row and 2 foll alt rows.
(51(51, 55, 55, 59, 59) sts)
Next row (WS) (dec): Sl1, P1, psso, K to last 2 sts, P2tog tbl.
Next row (WS) (dec): Sl1, K1, psso, K to last 2 sts, K2tog.
Cast off Kwise on **WS**.
Sew cast-on edge of collar around neck, starting
halfway across buttonhole band and ending halfway
across buttonband.
Place center of cast-off edge of sleeve to shoulder
seam. Set in sleeve, easing sleevehead into armhole.
Sew on buttons to correspond with buttonholes.

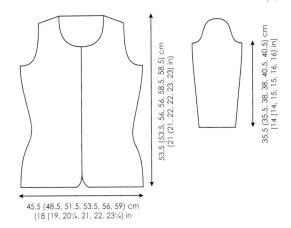

45.5 (48.5, 51.5, 53.5, 56, 59) cm
(18 (19, 20¼, 21, 22, 23¼) in

53.5 (53.5, 56, 56, 58.5, 58.5) cm
(21 (21, 22, 22, 23, 23) in)

35.5 (35.5, 38, 38, 40.5, 40.5) cm
(14 (14, 15, 15, 16, 16) in)

MARMEE

This classically tailored knitted jacket uses darts to create a very flattering silhouette. I suggest using stitch markers to mark the position of the darts. You can find some very pretty ones, which always enhance the knitting experience. This garment would work equally well in a wool or wool-blend, double knitting-weight yarn. I would suggest a straight yarn (not too much haze or fluff), or the lovely lines of the darts will get lost.

TO FIT DRESS SIZE:

8	10	12	14	16	18	**US**
10	12	14	16	18	20	**UK**
38	40	42	44	46	48	**EU**

ACTUAL SIZE: Ease allowance approx 7.5 cm (3 in)

90	95	101	106	112	117	cm
35½	37½	39¾	41¾	44	46	in

FINISHED LENGTH:

56	56	58	58	60	60	cm
22	22	22¾	22¾	23¾	23¾	in

SLEEVE LENGTH:

35.5	35.5	38	38	40.5	40.5	cm
14	14	15	15	16	16	in

YARN
Knitted in double knitting–weight yarn
1st size photographed in Louisa Harding Jasmine sh. 6 Pea

10	11	11	12	12	13	x 50g balls

NEEDLES
Pair of 3.25 mm (US 3) knitting needles
Pair of 4 mm (US 6) knitting needles

TENSION/GAUGE
22 sts x 30 rows to 10 cm (4 in) square measured over st st using 4 mm (US 6) knitting needles.

BUTTONS
6 medium mother of pearl buttons

BACK

Using 3.25 mm (US 3) needles cast on 99(105, 111, 117, 123, 129) sts.
Row 1: (K1, P1) to last st, K1.
Row 2: (K1, P1) to last st, K1.
These 2 rows form moss st.
Work in moss st for a further 6 rows.
Change to 4 mm (US 6) needles and beg with a K row work 8(8, 8, 10, 10, 10) rows in st st, ending with RS facing for next row.

SHAPE SIDE SEAMS AND DARTS
Place markers on 26th (27th, 28th, 29th, 30th, 31st) st counting in from each end of last row.
Next row (RS): (K to marked st, P marked st) twice, K to end.
Next row: (P to marked st, K marked st) twice, P to end.
Rep these 2 rows once more.
Next row (RS): K3, K2tog, (K to within 2 sts of marked st, K2tog, P1, K2tog tbl) twice, K to last 5 sts, K2tog tbl, K3.
(93(99, 105, 111, 117, 123) sts)
Work 11 rows in patt, keeping marked st correct.
Rep these 12 rows once more.
(87(93, 99, 105, 111, 117) sts)
Next row (RS): K3, K2tog, (K to within 2 sts of marked st, K2tog, P1, K2tog tbl) twice, K to last 5 sts, K2tog tbl, K3.
(81(87, 93, 99, 105, 111) sts)
Work 21 rows in patt, ending with RS facing for next row.
Next row (RS): K3, M1, (K to within 1 st of marked st, M1, K1, P1, K1, M1) twice, K to last 3 sts, M1, K3.
(87(93, 99, 105, 111, 117) sts)
Work 11 rows in patt keeping marked st correct.
Rep these 12 rows once more.
(93(99, 105, 111, 117, 123) sts)
Next row (RS): K3, M1, (K to within 1 st of marked st, M1, K1, P1, K1, M1) twice, K to last 3 sts, M1, K3.
(99(105, 111, 117, 123, 129) sts)
Beg with a P row cont in st st only until work measures 36(36, 37, 37, 38, 38) cm **(14¼(14¼, 14½, 14½, 15, 15) in)** from cast-on edge, ending with RS facing for next row.

SHAPE ARMHOLES
Cast off 4(5, 5, 6, 6, 7) sts at beg of next 2 rows.
(91(95, 101, 105, 111, 115) sts)
Next row (RS) (dec): K3, K2tog, K to last 5 sts, K2tog tbl, K3. (89(93, 99, 103, 109, 113) sts)
Next row (dec): P3, P2tog tbl, P to last 5 sts, P2tog, P3.
(87(91, 97, 101, 107, 111) sts)
Dec 1 st internally as above at each end of next 3(3, 5, 5, 7, 7) rows, then on 2(3, 3, 4, 4, 5) foll alt rows, then on every foll 4th row to 73(75, 77, 79, 81, 83) sts.
Cont without further shaping until armhole measures 20(20, 21, 21, 22, 22) cm **(8(8, 8¼, 8¼, 8¾, 8¾) in)**, ending with RS facing for next row.

SHAPE SHOULDERS
Cast off 7(7, 7, 7, 8, 8) sts at beg of next 2 rows.
(59(61, 63, 65, 65, 67] sts)

SHAPE RIGHT SHOULDER AND BACK NECK
Next row (RS): Cast off 7(7, 7, 7, 8, 8) sts, K until there are 11(11, 12, 12, 11, 12) sts on RH needle, turn and work this side first.
Cast off 4 sts at beg of next row.
Cast off rem 7(7, 8, 8, 7, 8) sts.
With RS facing, rejoin yarn to sts on holder, cast off center 23(25, 25, 27, 27, 27) sts, K to end.

SHAPE LEFT SHOULDER AND BACK NECK
Next row (WS): Cast off 7(7, 7, 7, 8, 8) sts, P to end.
Cast off 4 sts at beg of next row.
Cast off rem 7(7, 8, 8, 7, 8) sts.

LEFT FRONT

Using 3.25 mm (US 3) needles cast on 55(58, 61, 64, 67, 70) sts.
Row 1: (K1, P1) to last 1(2, 1, 2, 1, 2) sts, K1, P0(1, 0, 1, 0, 1).
Row 2: P0(1, 0, 1, 0, 1), (K1, P1) to last st, K1.
These 2 rows form moss st.
Work in moss st for a further 5 rows.
Row 8 (WS): Moss st 6 sts, slip these 6 sts onto a holder for buttonband, M1, moss st to end.
(50(53, 56, 59, 62, 65) sts)
Change to 4 mm (US 6) needles and beg with a K row work 8(8, 8, 10, 10, 10) rows in st st, ending with RS facing for next row.

SHAPE SIDE SEAM AND DART
Place marker on 26th (27th, 28th, 29th, 30th, 31st) st counting in from side seam of last row.
Next row (RS): K to marked st, P marked st, K to end.
Next row: P to marked st, K marked st, P to end.
Rep these 2 rows once more.
Next row (RS): K3, K2tog, K to within 2 sts of marked st, K2tog, P1, K2tog tbl, K to end. (47(50, 53, 56, 59, 62) sts)
Work 11 rows in patt, keeping marked st correct.
Rep these 12 rows once more. (44(47, 50, 53, 56, 59) sts)
Next row (RS): K3, K2tog, K to within 2 sts of marked st, K2tog, P1, K2tog tbl, K to end.
(41(44, 47, 50, 53, 56) sts)
Work 21 rows in patt, ending with RS facing for next row.
Next row (RS): K3, M1, K to within 1 st of marked st, M1, K1, P1, K1, M1, K to end. (44(47, 50, 53, 56, 59) sts)
Work 11 rows in patt, keeping marked st correct.
Rep these 12 rows once more. (47(50, 53, 56, 59, 62) sts)
Next row (RS): K3, M1, K to within 1 st of marked st, M1, K1, P1, K1, M1, K to end. (50(53, 56, 59, 62, 65) sts)
Beg with a P row cont in st st only until work measures 36(36, 37, 37, 38, 38) cm **(14¼(14¼, 14½, 14½, 15, 15) in)** from cast-on edge, ending with RS facing for next row.

SHAPE ARMHOLE AND FRONT NECK

Next row (RS): Cast off 4(5, 5, 6, 6, 7) sts, K to last 5 sts, K2tog tbl, K3. (45(47, 50, 52, 55, 57) sts)
Work 1 row.
Next row (RS) (dec): K3, K2tog, K to last 5 sts, K2tog tbl, K3. (43(45, 48, 50, 53, 55) sts)
Next row (dec): P to last 5 sts, P2tog, P3.
(42(44, 47, 49, 52, 54) sts)
Dec 1 st internally as above at armhole edge on next 3(3, 5, 5, 7, 7) rows, then 2(3, 3, 4, 4, 5) foll alt rows, then on 2 foll 4th rows, AT THE SAME TIME dec 1 st internally as above at neck edge on next and 2(4, 3, 5, 3, 3) foll alt rows, then on every foll 4th row. (30(29, 30, 30, 31, 32) sts.
Dec 1 st internally at neck edge only on every foll 4th row from previous dec until 21(21, 22, 22, 23, 24) sts rem.
Cont without further shaping until armhole measures 20(20, 21, 21, 22, 22) cm **(8(8, 8¼, 8¼, 8¾, 8¾) in)**, ending with RS facing for next row.

SHAPE SHOULDER

Cast off 7(7, 7, 7, 8, 8) sts at beg of next row and foll alt row.
Work 1 row.
Cast off rem 7(7, 8, 8, 7, 8) sts.

RIGHT FRONT

Using 3.25 mm (US 3) needles cast on 55(58, 61, 64, 67, 70) sts.
Row 1: P0(1, 0, 1, 0, 1), (K1, P1) to last st, K1.
Row 2: (K1, P1) to last 1(2, 1, 2, 1, 2) sts, K1, P0(1, 0, 1, 0, 1).
These 2 rows form moss st.
Work in moss st for a further 2 rows.
Row 5 (RS) (buttonhole): Moss st 1, patt 2tog, yo, moss st to end.
Work in moss st for a further 2 rows.
Row 8 (WS): Moss st to last 6 sts, M1 and turn, slip last 6 sts onto a holder for buttonhole band.
(50(53, 56, 59, 62, 65) sts)
Change to 4 mm (US 6) needles and beg with a K row work 8(8, 8, 10, 10, 10) rows in st st, ending with RS facing for next row.

SHAPE SIDE SEAM AND DART

Place marker on 26th (27th, 28th, 29th, 30th, 31st) st counting in from side seam of last row.
Next row (RS): K to marked st, P marked st, K to end.
Next row: P to marked st, K marked st, P to end.
Rep these 2 rows once more.
Next row (RS): K to within 2 sts of marked st, K2tog, P1, K2tog tbl, K to last 5 sts, K2tog tbl, K3.
(47(50, 53, 56, 59, 62) sts)
Work 11 rows in patt, keeping marked st correct.
Rep these 12 rows once more. (44(47, 50, 53, 56, 59) sts)
Next row (RS): K to within 2 sts of marked st, K2tog, P1, K2tog tbl, K to last 5 sts, K2tog tbl, K3.
(41(44, 47, 50, 53, 56) sts)

Work 21 rows in patt, ending with RS facing for next row.
Next row (RS): K to within 1 st of marked st, M1, K1, P1, K1, M1, K to last 3 sts, M1, K3. (44(47, 50, 53, 56, 59) sts)
Work 11 rows in patt, keeping marked st correct.
Rep these 12 rows once more. (47(50, 53, 56, 59, 62) sts)
Next row (RS): K to within 1 st of marked st, M1, K1, P1, K1, M1, K to last 5 sts, M1, K3. (50(53, 56, 59, 62, 65) sts)
Beg with a P row cont in st st only until work measures 36(36, 37, 37, 38, 38) cm **(14¼(14¼, 14½, 14½, 15, 15) in)** from cast on edge, ending with RS facing for next row.

SHAPE ARMHOLE AND FRONT NECK

Next row (RS) (dec): K3, K2tog, K to end.
(49(52, 55, 58, 61, 64) sts)
Next row (WS) (dec): Cast off 4(5, 5, 6, 6, 7) sts, P to end.
(45(47, 50, 52, 55, 57) sts)
Next row (RS) (dec): K3, K2tog, K to last 5 sts, K2tog tbl, K3. (43(45, 48, 50, 53, 55) sts)
Next row (dec): P3, P2tog tbl, P to end.
(42(44, 47, 49, 52, 54) sts)
Dec 1 st internally as above at armhole edge on next 3(3, 5, 5, 7, 7) rows, then on 2(3, 3, 4, 4, 5) foll alt rows, then on 2 foll 4th rows, **at the same time** dec 1 st internally as above at neck edge on next and 2(4, 3, 5, 3, 3) foll alt rows, then on every foll 4th row. (30(29, 30, 30, 31, 32) sts.
Dec 1 st internally at neck edge only until 21(21, 22, 22, 23, 24) sts rem.
Cont without further shaping until armhole measures 20(20, 21, 21, 22, 22) cm **(8(8, 8¼, 8¼, 8¾, 8¾) in)**, ending with RS facing for next row.

SHAPE SHOULDER

Cast off 7(7, 7, 7, 8, 8) sts at beg of next row and foll alt row.
Work 1 row.
Cast off rem 7(7, 8, 8, 7, 8) sts.

SLEEVES (work both the same)

Using 3.25 mm (US 3) needles cast on 57(57, 59, 59, 61, 61) sts.
Row 1: (K1, P1) to last st, K1.
Row 2: (K1, P1) to last st, K1.
These 2 rows form moss st.
Work in moss st for a further 6 rows.
Change to 4 mm (US 6) needles and beg with a K row work 4 rows in st st, ending with RS facing for next row.
Next row (RS) (inc): K3, M1, K to last 3 sts, M1, K3.
(59(59, 61, 61, 63, 63) sts)
Beg with a P row work 9 rows in st st, ending with RS facing for next row.
Working all incs internally as above inc at each end of next row and every foll 10th row to 73(73, 77, 77, 81, 81) sts.
Cont without further shaping until work measures 35.5(35.5, 38, 38, 40.5, 40.5) cm, **(14(14, 15, 15, 16, 16) in)** from cast on edge, ending with RS facing for next row.

SHAPE SLEEVEHEAD

Cast off 4(4, 5, 5, 6, 6) sts at beg of next 2 rows.
(65(65, 67, 67, 69, 69) sts)
Dec 1 st at each end of next row and 4 foll rows.
(55(55, 57, 57, 59, 59) sts)
Work 1 row.
Dec 1 st at each end of next row and foll alt row.
(51(51, 53, 53, 55, 55) sts)
Work 3 rows.
Dec 1 st at each end of next row and 4 foll 4th rows.
(41(41, 43, 43, 45, 45) sts)
Work 1 row.
Dec 1 st at each end of next row and every foll alt row to 37 sts, then at each end of next 3 rows. (31 sts)
Cast off 4 sts at beg of next 4 rows.
Cast off rem 15 sts.

MAKING UP

Press/block as described in finishing techniques (pg 158).
Join both shoulder seams.
Place a marker 9 cm (3½ in) down from shoulder seams at each side of front neck.

BUTTONBAND AND LEFT COLLAR

With RS facing, slip 6 sts from left front holder onto 3.25 mm (US 3) needle, rejoin yarn and work in moss st until buttonband fits up left front to start of neck shaping when slightly stretched, stitching band into place as you work and ending with RS facing for next row.

SHAPE COLLAR

Next row (RS of front, WS of collar): Moss st 1, K into front, back, front of next st, moss st to end. (8 sts)
Work 5 rows.
Rep the last 6 rows 6 times more. (20 sts)
Cont straight until collar unstretched fits up left front slope to marker, ending at collar outside edge, stitching into place as you work.

Next row: Cast off 9 sts, turn, cast on 9 sts (for notch in collar), moss st to end.
Cont in moss st until collar fits up left front to shoulder, and across to center back neck, stitching into place as you work.
Cast off in moss st.
Mark the position of 6 buttons on buttonband, the first to come opposite buttonhole made in right front band, the last to be positioned at start of front neck shaping.

BUTTONHOLE BAND AND RIGHT COLLAR

With **WS** facing, slip 6 sts from right front holder onto 3.25 mm (US 3) needle, rejoin yarn and work in moss st until buttonhole band fits up left front to start of neck shaping when slightly stretched, AT THE SAME TIME work buttonholes to match positions marked for buttons as folls:
Buttonhole row (RS): Moss st 1, patt 2 tog, yo, moss st 3.
Slip stitch band into place as you work and end with RS facing for next row.

SHAPE COLLAR

Next row (RS of front, WS of collar): Moss st to last 2 sts, K into front, back, front of next st, moss st 1. (8 sts)
Work 5 rows.
Rep the last 6 rows 6 times more. (20 sts)
Cont straight until collar (unstretched) fits up left front slope to marker, ending at collar outside edge, stitching into place as you work.
Next row: Cast off 9 sts, turn, cast on 9 sts (for notch in collar), moss st to end.
Cont in moss st until collar fits up left front to shoulder, and across to center back neck, stitching into place as you work.
Cast off in moss st.
Join collar at back neck.
Join side and sleeve seams.
Place center of cast-off edge of sleeves to shoulder seams. Set in sleeves using the set-in method, easing sleeveheads into armholes.
Sew on buttons to correspond with buttonholes.

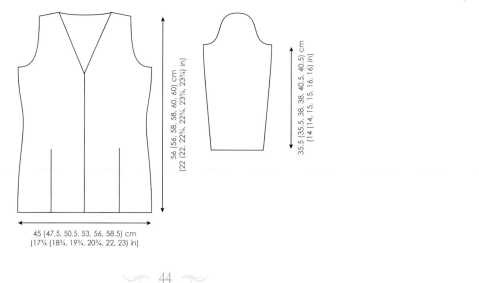

56 (56, 58, 58, 60, 60) cm
(22 (22, 22¾, 22¾, 23¾, 23¾) in)

45 (47.5, 50.5, 53, 56, 58.5) cm
(17¾ (18¾, 19¾, 20¾, 22, 23) in)

35.5 (35.5, 38, 38, 40.5, 40.5) cm
(14 (14, 15, 15, 16, 16) in)

Edgings

Adding an edging to your garment takes your knitting skill to another level, mainly because it forces you to experiment with design. While the patterns are very straightforward, the edgings dazzle, using lace or cable stitches and contrasting or complementary yarns. So go ahead: take a simple cardigan pattern and mix and match the different edgings here. Finally, feel free to choose a completely different shade or yarn from the main body for a totally unique-to-you look.

TIDE

This design originally came from my collection inspired by beachcombing and was photographed on the beach in the south of France. This is a fun little cardigan with the easiest edging. Worked at the beginning of the pattern, the undulating hem is achieved by yarn-over eyelets and knitting stitches together, and the resulting design looks like a wave. We remade and re-photographed it using a different yarn with more drape, and in this second version I decided to show it with a ribbon tied at the waist, making for a very feminine silhouette.

TO FIT DRESS SIZE:

8–10	12–14	16–18	**US**
10–12	14–16	18–20	**UK**
38–40	42–44	46–48	**EU**

ACTUAL SIZE: Ease allowance approx 5–10 cm (2-4 in)

92	110	128	cm
36¼	43¼	50½	in

FINISHED LENGTH:

40	43	46	cm
15¾	17	18	in

SLEEVE LENGTH:

8.5	8.5	8.5	cm
3¼	3¼	3¼	in

YARN

Knitted in worsted–weight yarn
1st size photographed in Louisa Harding Glisten sh. 4 Golden

8	9	10	x 50g balls

2nd size photographed in Louisa Harding Albero sh. 2 Oyster

5	6	7	x 50g balls

NEEDLES

Pair of 4 mm (US 6) knitting needles
Pair of 5 mm (US 8) knitting needles
4 mm (US 6) circular needle

EXTRAS

1 medium shell button
2 meters (79 in) x 1.3 cm (½ in) ribbon

TENSION/GAUGE

20 sts x 28 rows to 10 cm (4 in) square measured over st st using 5 mm (US 8) knitting needles

Back

Using 4 mm (US 6) needles cast on 92(110, 128) sts.
Row 1 (RS): Knit.
Row 2: Knit.
These 2 rows form garter st.
Work in garter st for a further 2 rows.
Change to 5 mm (US 8) needles and work 4 row textured pattern as folls:
Row 1 (RS): Knit.
Row 2: Purl.
Row 3: K1, [(K2tog) 3 times, (yo, K1) 6 times, (K2tog) 3 times] 5(6, 7) times, K1.
Row 4: Knit.
Cont to work in scallop patt until work measures 10 cm **(4 in)**, ending with RS facing for next row.
Beg with a K row work in st st only until work measures 22(24, 26) cm **(8¾(9½, 10¼) in)**, ending with RS facing for next row.

Shape armholes

Cast off 4(6, 7) sts at beg next 2 rows, and 3(3, 4) sts at beg foll 2 rows. (78(92, 106) sts)
Dec 1 st at armhole edge on next 3(5, 5) rows and 2(4, 6) foll alt rows. (68(74, 84) sts)
Cont without further shaping until armhole measures 18(19, 20) cm **(7(7½, 8) in)** ending with RS facing for next row.

Shape back neck and shoulders

Cast off 6(7, 9) sts at beg next 2 rows.
Cast off 6(7, 9) sts beg next row, K until there are 9(10, 11) sts on RH needle, turn, work both side of neck separately.
Cast off 3 sts, P to end.
Cast off rem 6(7, 8) sts.
Rejoin yarn to rem sts, cast off center 26 sts, K to end.
Complete to match first side, reversing shapings.

Left front

Using 4 mm (US 6) needles cast on 47(56, 65) sts.
Row 1 (RS): Knit.
Row 2: Knit.
These 2 rows form garter st.
Work in garter st for a further 2 rows.
Change to 5 mm (US 8) needles and work 4 row textured pattern as folls:
Row 1 (RS): Knit.
Row 2: Purl.

Small & large sizes only

Row 3: K1, [(K2tog) 3 times, (yo, K1) 6 times, (K2tog) 3 times] 2(3) times, (K2tog) 3 times, (K1, yo) 3 times, K1.

Medium size only

Row 3: K1, [(K2tog) 3 times, (yo, K1) 6 times, (K2tog) 3 times] 3 times, K1.

All sizes

Row 4: Knit.
Cont to work in scallop patt until work measures 10 cm **(4 in)**, ending with RS facing for next row.
Beg with a K row work in st st only until work measures 22(24, 26) cm **(8¾(9½, 10¼) in)**, ending with RS facing for next row.

Shape armhole and front neck

Next row (RS) (dec): Cast off 4(6, 7) sts at beg next row, K to last 2 sts, K2tog. (42(49, 57) sts)
Work 1 row.
Next row (RS) (dec): Cast off 3(3, 4) sts at beg next row, K to last 2 sts, K2tog. (38(45, 52) sts)
Work 1 row.
Dec 1 st at armhole edge on next 3(5, 5) rows and 2(4, 6) foll alt rows, and **at the same time** dec 1 st at neck edge as sts set on every alt row, ending with RS facing for next row. (29(29, 32) sts)
Cont to dec at neck edge on next 5(1, 0) foll alt rows. (24(28, 32) sts)
Work 3 rows.
Dec 1 st at neck edge on next row and every foll 4th row until 18(21, 26) sts rem.
Cont without further shaping until armhole measures 18(19, 20) cm **(7(7½, 8) in)** ending with RS facing for next row.

Shape shoulder

Cast off 6(7, 9) sts at beg next row and foll alt row.
Work 1 row.
Cast off rem 6(7, 8) sts.

Right front

Using 4 mm (US 6) needles cast on 47(56, 65) sts.
Row 1 (RS): Knit.
Row 2: Knit.
These 2 rows form garter st.
Work in garter st for a further 2 rows.
Change to 5 mm (US 8) needles and work 4 row textured pattern as folls:
Row 1 (RS): Knit.
Row 2: Purl.

Small & large sizes only

Row 3: K1, (yo, K1) 3 times, (K2tog) 3 times, [(K2tog) 3 times, (yo, K1) 6 times, (K2tog) 3 times] 2(3) times, K1.

Medium size only

Row 3: K1, [(K2tog) 3 times, (yo, K1) 6 times, (K2tog) 3 times] 3 times, K1.

All sizes

Row 4: Knit.
Cont to work in striped scallop patt until work measures 10 cm **(4 in)**, ending with RS facing for next row.

Complete to match left front, reversing shapings and working an extra row before beg armhole and shoulder shaping.

Sleeves (work both the same)

Using 4 mm (US 6) needles cast on 56(60, 64) sts.
Row 1 (RS): Knit.
Row 2: Knit.
These 2 rows form garter st.
Work in garter st for a further 2 rows.
Change to 5 mm (US 8) needles and work 4 row textured pattern as folls:
Row 1 (RS): Knit.
Row 2: Purl.
Row 3: K1(3, 5), [(K2tog) 3 times, (yo, K1) 6 times, (K2tog) 3 times] 3 times, K1(3, 5).
Row 4: Knit.
Work these 4 rows once more.
Cont to work in st st only inc 1 st at each end of next row and foll 4th row. (60(64, 68) sts)
Work without further shaping until work measures 8.5 cm **(3¼ in)**, ending with RS facing for next row.

Shape sleevehead

Cast off 4(5, 6) sts at beg next 2 rows. (52(54, 56) sts)
Dec 1 st at each end of next 3 rows and 3 foll alt rows. (40(42, 44) sts)
Work 3 rows.
Dec1 st at each end of next row and 3 foll 4th rows. (32(34, 36) sts)
Work 1 row.
Dec 1 st at each end of next row and foll alt row, then every row until 22(24, 26) sts rem.
Cast off 3 sts at beg next 4 rows. (10(12, 14) sts)
Cast off.

Making up

Press/block as described in finishing techniques (pg 158). Join both shoulder seams.

Front edging (worked in one piece)
With RS facing and using 4 mm (US 6) circular needle and yarn A, pick up and K 21 sts from scallop edge, 21(23, 25) sts to start of front neck shaping, 38(40, 42) sts to shoulder, 32 sts across back neck, 38(40, 42) sts down to start of front neck, 21(23, 25) sts to edging and 21 sts from scallop edging. (192(200, 208) sts)
Work 2 rows in garter st.
Cast off Kwise on **WS**.
Join side and sleeve seams.
Place center of cast-off edge of sleeves to shoulder seams. Set in sleeves using the set-in method, easing sleeveheads into armholes.
Make a button loop: Use 1 strand of yarn A and make 1 x 6.5 cm **(2½ in)** length of chain cording—with a slip knot in right hand, *pull yarn through to make a new slip knot, rep from * until chain is the reqired length. This takes a little practice to get an even tension.
Sew button loop into place at start of neck shaping on right front. Sew on button to correspond with button loop on left front, alternatively thread ribbon starting at right front opening thread ribbon through eyelet pattern created by last pattern repeat of scallop edging, thread across back and left front to left front opening.
Tie in a bow. ✑

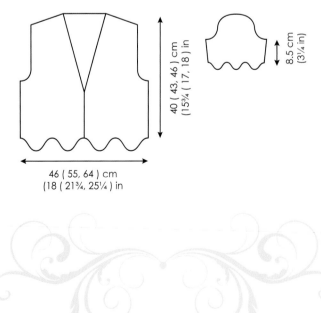

40 (43, 46) cm
(15¾ (17, 18) in

8.5 cm
(3¼ in)

46 (55, 64) cm
(18 (21¾, 25¼) in

MUSE

This elegant little cardigan is simple in construction. I wanted to use the softest of yarns and opted for a lovely variegated angora. I highlighted one of the colors and used a ribbon yarn for the edgings, which are sewn on once the garment is completed. Alternatively this design could be knitted using a single yarn in one color (for both body and edging) for a more uniform-looking garment.

TO FIT DRESS SIZE:

8	10	12	14	16	18	**US**
10	12	14	16	18	20	**UK**
38	40	42	44	46	48	**EU**

ACTUAL SIZE: Ease allowance approx 5 cm (2 in)

86	90	97	103	106	110	cm
34	35½	38¼	40½	41¾	43¼	in

FINISHED LENGTH:

43	43	45.5	45.5	48.5	48.5	cm
17	17	18	18	19	19	in

SLEEVE LENGTH:

40.5	40.5	42	42	43	43	cm
16	16	16½	16½	17	17	in

YARN

Knitted in double knitting–weight yarn
1st size photographed in Louisa Harding Kimono Angora
and Kimono Ribbon Pure
A. Kimono Angora sh. 9 Pink Shell

5	5	6	6	6	7	x 25g balls

B. Kimono Ribbon Pure sh. 1 Rice

2	2	2	3	3	3	x 50g balls

NEEDLES

Pair of 4 mm (US 6) knitting needles
Pair of 5.5 mm (US 9) knitting needles

BUTTON

1 medium mother of pearl

TENSION/GAUGE

22 sts x 30 rows to 10cm (4 in) square measured over st st using 4 mm (US 6) knitting needles and yarn A

Back

Using 4 mm (US 6) needles and yarn A cast on 87(91, 99, 105, 109, 113) sts.
Beg with a K row work 10 rows in st st.
Next row (RS) (inc): K3, M1, K to last 3 sts, M1, K3.
(89(93, 101, 107, 111, 115) sts)
Work 9 rows in st st.
Inc 1 st as above on next row and 2 foll 10th rows to 95(99, 107, 113, 117, 121) sts.
Cont without further shaping until work measures 19(19, 20.5, 20.5, 22.5, 22.5)cm **(7½(7½, 8, 8, 9, 9)in)** from cast on ending with RS facing for next row.

Shape armholes

Cast off 4(5, 7, 9, 9, 9) sts at beg next 2 rows and 3(3, 3, 3, 4, 4) sts at beg 2 foll rows. (81(83, 87, 89, 91, 95) sts)
Next row (RS) (dec): K3, K2tog, K to last 5 sts, K2tog tbl, K3. (79(81, 85, 87, 89, 93) sts)
Work 1 row.
Dec 1 st as above on next row and 3(3, 4, 4, 4, 4) foll alt rows. (71(73, 75, 77, 79, 83) sts)
Work without further shaping until work measures 18(18, 19, 19, 20, 20)cm **(7(7, 7½, 7½, 8, 8)in)** from armhole, ending with RS facing for next row.

Shape shoulders and back neck

Cast off 6(7, 7, 7, 7, 8) sts at the beg next 2 rows.
Cast off 6(7, 7, 7, 7, 8) sts, K until 10(9, 9, 10, 10, 10) sts remain on needle, turn, leave rem sts on a holder.
Cast off 3 sts, P to end.
Cast off rem 7(6, 6, 7, 7, 7) sts.
Rejoin yarn to rem sts, cast off center 27(27, 29, 29, 31, 31) sts, K to end.
Complete to match first side reversing shapings.

Left front

Using 4 mm (US 6) needles and yarn A cast on 24(26, 30, 33, 35, 37) sts.
Beg with a K row work 2 rows in st st.
Next row (RS) (inc): K to last 3 sts, M1, K3.
(25(27, 31, 34, 36, 38) sts)
Work 1 row.
Inc 1 st as above on next row and 2 foll alt rows. (28(30, 34, 37, 39, 41) sts)
Work 1 row.
Next row (RS) (inc): K3, M1, K to end.
(29(31, 35, 38, 40, 42) sts)
Work 1 row.
Next row (RS) (inc): K to last 3 sts, M1, K3.
(30(32, 36, 39, 41, 43) sts)
Work 3 rows.
Next row (RS) (inc): K to last 3 sts, M1, K3.
(31(33, 37, 40, 42, 44) sts)
Work 3 rows.
Next row (RS) (inc): K3, M1, K to last 3 sts, M1, K3.

(33(35, 39, 42, 44, 46) sts)
Work 9 rows in st st.
Inc 1 st as above at side edge only on next row and foll 10th row. (35(37, 41, 44, 46, 48) sts)
Cont without further shaping until work measures 19(19, 20.5, 20.5, 22.5, 22.5)cm **(7½(7½, 8, 8, 9, 9)in)** from cast on ending with RS facing for next row.

Shape armhole

Cast off 4(5, 7, 9, 9, 9) sts at beg next row and 3(3, 3, 3, 4, 4) sts at beg foll alt row. (28(29, 31, 32, 33, 35) sts)
Work 1 row.
Next row (RS) (dec): K3, K2tog, K to end.
(27(28, 30, 31, 32, 34) sts)
Work 1 row.
Dec 1 st as above on next row and 3(3, 4, 4, 4, 4) foll alt rows. (23(24, 25, 26, 27, 29) sts)
Work without further shaping until front is 10 rows shorter than back to shoulder shaping, ending with RS facing for next row.

Shape front neck

Dec 1 st at neck edge on next 4(4, 5, 5, 6, 6) rows.
(19(20, 20, 21, 21, 23) sts)
Work until front matches back to shoulder, ending with RS facing for next row.

Shape shoulder

Cast off 6(7, 7, 7, 7, 8) sts at beg next row and foll alt row.
Work 1 row.
Cast off rem 7(6, 6, 7, 7, 7) sts.

Right front

Using 4 mm (US 6) needles and yarn A cast on 24(26, 30, 33, 35, 37) sts.
Beg with a K row work 2 rows in st st.
Next row (RS) (inc): K3, M1, K to end.
(25(27, 31, 34, 36, 38) sts)
Work 1 row.
Inc 1 st as above on next row and 2 foll alt rows.
(28(30, 34, 37, 39, 41) sts)
Work 1 row.
Next row (RS) (inc): K to last 3 sts, M1, K3.
(29(31, 35, 38, 40, 42) sts)
Work 1 row.
Next row (RS) (inc): K3, M1, K to end.
(30(32, 36, 39, 41, 43) sts)
Work 3 rows.
Next row (RS) (inc): K3, M1, K to end.
(31(33, 37, 40, 42, 44) sts)
Work 3 rows.
Next row (RS) (inc): K3, M1, K to last 3 sts, M1, K3.
(33(35, 39, 42, 44, 46) sts)
Work 9 rows in st st.
Inc 1 st as above at side edge only on next row and foll 10th row. (35(37, 41, 44, 46, 48) sts)

Cont without further shaping until work measures 19(19, 20.5, 20.5, 22.5, 22.5)cm **(7½(7½, 8, 8, 9, 9)in)** from cast on ending with **WS** facing for next row.

SHAPE ARMHOLE
Cast off 4(5, 7, 9, 9, 9) sts at beg next row and 3(3, 3, 3, 4, 4) sts at beg foll alt row. (28(29, 31, 32, 33, 35 sts)
Next row (RS) (dec): K to last 5 sts, K2tog tbl, K3. (27(28, 30, 31, 32, 34) sts)
Work 1 row.
Dec 1 st as above on next row and 3(3, 4, 4, 4, 4) foll alt rows. (23(24, 25, 26, 27, 29) sts)
Work without further shaping until front is 10 rows shorter than back to shoulder shaping, ending with RS facing for next row.

SHAPE FRONT NECK
Dec 1 st at neck edge on next 4(4, 5, 5, 6, 6) rows. (19(20, 20, 21, 21, 23) sts)
Work until front matches back to shoulder ending with **WS** facing for next row.

SHAPE SHOULDER
Cast off 6(7, 7, 7, 7, 8) sts at beg next row and foll alt row.
Work 1 row.
Cast off rem 7(6, 6, 7, 7, 7) sts.

SLEEVES (work both the same)

Using 4 mm (US 6) needles and yarn A cast on 55(55, 57, 57, 59, 59) sts.
Beg with a K row work 10 rows in st st.
Inc 1 st at each end of next row and every foll 10th row to 67(67, 71, 71, 75, 75) sts.
Work without further shaping until work measures 30.5(30.5, 32, 32, 33, 33) cm **(12(12, 12¾, 12¾, 13, 13)in)** from cast-on edge, ending with RS facing for next row.

SHAPE SLEEVEHEAD
Cast off 5 sts at beg next 2 rows and 3 sts at beg 2 foll rows. (51(51, 55, 55, 59, 59) sts)
Dec 1 st at each end of next 3 rows and 3 foll alt rows. (39(39, 43, 43, 47, 47) sts)
Work 3 rows.
Dec 1 st at each end of next row and 3 foll 4th rows. (31(31, 35, 35, 39, 39) sts)
Work 1 row.
Dec 1 st at each end of next row and 2 foll alt rows, then on every row until 19(19, 23, 23, 27, 27) sts rem, ending with RS facing for next row.
Cast off 3 sts beg next 4 rows.
Cast off rem 7(7, 11, 11, 15, 15) sts.

MAKING UP

Press/block as described in finishing techniques (pg 158).
Join both shoulder seams and side seams using back stitch.

LACE EDGING
Using 5.5 mm (US 9) needles and yarn B cast on 11 sts and work 4 row lace edging as follows:
Row 1 (RS): K3, yo, K2tog tbl, K1, K2tog, yo, K3.
Row 2: K2, P7, K2.
Row 3: K4, yo, sl1, K2tog, psso, yo, K4.
Row 4: K2, P7, K2.
Rep these 4 rows until lace edging fits around edge of bolero from front neck to front neck.
Slip st into place.

SLEEVE LACE EDGING (work both the same)
Using 5.5 mm (US 9) needles and yarn B cast on 18 sts and work 4 row lace edging as follows:
Row 1 (RS): K10, yo, K2tog tbl, K1, K2tog, yo, K3.
Row 2: K2, P7, K9.
Row 3: K11, yo, sl1, K2tog, psso, yo, K4.
Row 4: K2, P7, K9.
Rep these 4 rows until lace edging fits until edging fits around base of sleeve, slip st into place.

NECKBAND
With RS facing of right front and using 5.5 mm (US 9) needles and yarn B, pick up and K 11 sts from lace edging, 10(10, 12, 12, 14, 14) sts to shoulder, 26(26, 28, 28, 30, 30) sts across back neck and 10(10, 12, 12, 14, 14) sts down left front neck to edging, pick up and K11 sts from edging. (68(68, 74, 74, 80, 80) sts)
Work 2 rows in garter st.
Cast off Kwise on **WS**.
Join sleeve seams.
Place center of cast-off edge of sleeve to shoulder seam. Set in sleeve, easing sleevehead into armhole.

MAKE BUTTON LOOP
Use 1 strand of yarn B and make a 6 cm **(2½ in)** length of chain cording —with a slip knot in right hand, *pull yarn through to make a new slip knot, rep from * until chain is the reqired length. This takes a little practice to get an even tension. Sew button loop into place at start of neck shaping on right front.
Sew on button to correspond with button loop.

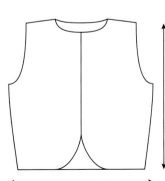

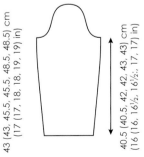

43 (43, 45.5, 45.5, 48.5, 48.5) cm
(17 (17, 18, 18, 19, 19) in)

43 (45, 48.5, 51.5, 53, 55) cm
(17 (17¾, 19, 20¼, 21, 21¾) in)

40.5 (40.5, 42, 42, 43, 43) cm
(16 (16, 16½, 16½, 17, 17) in)

GINGER

This cardigan has a very 1950s swing feel to it, and the plaited cable edging gives the garment stability and flair. A single button fastens at the neck; alternatively you could use a brooch and fasten the garment anywhere along the fronts. Knitted here in an aran-weight yarn, it would also look great in a tweed, changing the feel entirely.

To fit dress size:

8	10	12	14	16	18	**US**
10	12	14	16	18	20	**UK**
38	40	42	44	46	48	**EU**

Actual size: Ease allowance approx 10 cm (4 in)

90	97	101	108	112	117	cm
35½	38¼	39¾	42½	44	46	in

Finished length:

51	51	53.5	53.5	56	56	cm
20	20	21	21	22	22	in

Sleeve length:

35.5	35.5	38	38	40.5	40.5	cm
14	14	15	15	16	16	in

Yarn
Knitted in aran-weight yarn
2nd size photographed in Louisa Harding Kashmir Aran
sh. 17 Brick

12	13	14	15	16	17	x 50g balls

Needles
Pair of 4 mm (US 6) knitting needles
Pair of 5 mm (US 8) knitting needles
Cable needle

Button
1 large button

Tension/gauge
18 sts x 24 rows to 10cm/4in square measured over
st st using 5 mm (US 8) knitting needles

Back

Using 4 mm (US 6) needles cast on 81(87, 91, 97, 101, 105) sts.
Next row (RS): (K1, P1) to last st, K1.
Next row: (K1, P1) to last st, K1.
These 2 rows form moss st.
Work 16 more rows in moss st.
Change to 5 mm (US 8) needles and beg with a K row work in st st until work measures 33(33, 34.5, 34.5, 36, 36) cm **(13(13, 13½, 13½, 14, 14)in)** from cast-on edge, ending with RS facing for next row.

Shape armholes

Cast off 3(5, 6, 7, 7, 8) sts at beg next 2 rows and 3(3, 3, 4, 4, 4) sts beg 2 foll rows. (69(71, 73, 75, 79, 81) sts)
Dec 1 st at both ends of next row and 2(2, 2, 2, 3, 3) foll alt rows. (63(65, 67, 69, 71, 73) sts)
Work without further shaping until work measures 18(18, 19, 19, 20, 20) cm **(7(7, 7½, 7½, 8, 8)in)** from armhole, ending with RS facing for next row.

Shape shoulders and back neck

Cast off 5(5, 5, 6, 6, 6) sts beg next 2 rows.
Cast off 5(5, 5, 6, 6, 6) sts, K until there are 8(9, 9, 8, 8, 9) sts on RH needle and turn, leaving rem sts on a holder.
Work both sides of neck separately.
Cast off 3 sts, P to end.
Cast off rem 5(6, 6, 5, 5, 6) sts.
With RS rejoin yarn to rem sts, cast off 27(27, 29, 29, 31, 31) sts, K to end.
Complete to match first side, reversing shapings.

Left front

Using 4 mm (US 6) needles cast on 42(45, 47, 50, 52, 54) sts.
Next row (RS): P0(1, 1, 0, 0, 0), (K1, P1) to end.
Next row: (P1, K1) to last st, P0(1, 1, 0, 0, 0).
These 2 rows form moss st.
Work 15 more rows in moss st, ending with **WS** facing for next row.
Next row (WS): Patt 11 sts, leave these on a holder, patt to end. (31(34, 36, 39, 41, 43) sts)
Change to 5 mm (US 8) needles and beg with a K row work in st st until work measures 33(33, 34.5, 34.5, 36, 36) cm **(13(13, 13½, 13½, 14, 14)in)** from cast on edge, ending with RS facing for next row.

Shape armhole

Cast off 3(5, 6, 7, 7, 8) sts at beg next row and 3(3, 3, 4, 4, 4) sts beg foll alt row. (25(26, 27, 28, 30, 31) sts)
Work 1 row.
Dec 1 st at beg next row and 2(2, 2, 2, 3, 3) foll alt rows. (22(23, 24, 25, 26, 27) sts)
Work without further shaping until front is 11 rows shorter than back to shoulder, ending with **WS** facing for next row.

Shape front neck

Cast off 4(4, 5, 5, 6, 6) sts at beg next row. (18(19, 19, 20, 20, 21) sts)
Dec 1 st at neck edge on next 3 rows. (15(16, 16, 17, 17, 18) sts)
Work until front matches back to shoulder, ending with RS facing for next row.

Shape shoulder

Cast off 5(5, 5, 6, 6, 6) sts beg next row and foll alt row.
Work 1 row.
Cast off rem 5(6, 6, 5, 5, 6) sts.

Right front

Using 4 mm (US 6) needles cast on 42(45, 47, 50, 52, 54) sts.
Next row (RS): P0(1, 1, 0, 0, 0), (K1, P1) to end.
Next row: (P1, K1) to last st, P0(1, 1, 0, 0, 0).
These 2 rows form moss st.
Work 16 more rows in moss st, ending with RS facing for next row.
Change to 5 mm (US 8) needles.
Next row (RS): Patt 11 sts, leave these on a holder, K to end. (31(34, 36, 39, 41, 43) sts)
Beg with a purl row work in st st until work measures 33(33, 34.5, 34.5, 36, 36) cm **(13(13, 13½, 13½, 14, 14)in)** from cast-on edge, ending with **WS** facing for next row.
Complete to match left front, reversing shapings and working an extra row before beg armhole, neck, and shoulder shaping.

Sleeves (work both the same)

Using 5 mm (US 8) needles cast on 69(69, 73, 73, 77, 77) sts.
Beg with a K row work 10 rows in st st.
Dec 1 st at each end of next row and every foll 10th row to 57(57, 61, 61, 65, 65) sts.
Work without further shaping until work measures 29.5(29.5, 32, 32, 34.5, 34.5) cm **(11½(11½, 12¾, 12¾, 13½, 13½)in)** from cast-on edge, ending with RS facing for next row.

Shape sleevehead

Cast off 5 sts at beg next 2 rows. (47(47, 51, 51, 55, 55) sts)
Dec 1 st at each end of next 3 rows and 3 foll alt rows. (35(35, 39, 39, 43, 43) sts)
Work 3 rows.
Dec1 st at each end of next row and 2 foll 4th rows. (29(29, 33, 33, 37, 37) sts)
Work 1 row.
Dec 1 st at each end of next row and 2 foll alt rows, then on foll row. (21(21, 25, 25, 29, 29) sts)
Cast off 3 sts at beg next 4 rows.
Cast off rem 9(9, 13, 13, 17, 17) sts.

Making up

Press/block as described in finishing techniques (pg 158). Join both shoulder seams using back stitch.

Left front band
With RS facing and using 4 mm (US 6) needles, cast on 1 st, rejoin yarn to sts on holder for left front band and patt across 3 sts in moss st, K2, (M1, K1) 3 times, patt 3 sts in moss st. (15 sts)
Next row (WS): Moss st 3, P8, moss st 4.
Work 6 rows in cable edging as folls:
Edging row 1(RS): Moss st 4, K8, moss st 3.
Edging row 2 and every alt row: Moss st 3, P8, moss st 4.
Edging row 3: Moss st 4, C4B, C4F, moss st 3.
Edging row 5: Moss st 4, K8, moss st 3.
Edging row 6: Moss st 3, P8, moss st 4.
Rep these 6 rows until edging fits up to front neck shaping, leave sts on a holder.
Stitch into place using mattress stitch or back stitch if preferred.

Right front band
With **WS** facing and using 4 mm (US 6) needles, cast on 1 st, rejoin yarn to sts on holder for right front band and patt across 3 sts in moss st, P1, (M1, P1) 3 times, P1, patt 3 sts in moss st. (15 sts)
Work 6 rows in cable edging as folls:
Edging row 1 (RS): Moss st 3, K8, moss st 4.
Edging row 2 and every alt row: Moss st 4, P8, moss st 3.
Edging row 3: Moss st 3, C4B, C4F, moss st 4.
Edging row 5: Moss st 3, K8, moss st 4.
Edging row 6: Moss st 4, P8, moss st 3.
Rep these 6 rows until edging fits up to front neck shaping, leave sts on a holder.
Stitch into place using mattress stitch or back stitch if preferred.

Neck band
With RS of right front facing and using 4 mm (US 6) needles, patt across sts on holder as folls: K3, (K2tog, K1) twice, K2tog, K2, K2tog, pick up and K 14(14, 15, 15, 16, 16) sts to shoulder, 33(33, 35, 35, 37, 37) sts across back neck and 14(14, 15, 15, 16, 16) sts down left front neck to sts on holder, K2tog, K2, (K2tog, K1)twice, K2tog, K3. (83(83, 87, 87, 91, 91) sts)
Knit 2 rows.
Cast off Kwise on **WS**.

Sleeve edging (work both the same)
Using 4 mm (US 6) needles cast on 12 sts.
Foundation row: Moss st 3, K2, (M1, K1) 3 times, moss st 4. (15 sts)
Work 6 rows in cable edging as folls:
Edging row 1 (RS): Moss st 4, K8, moss st 3.
Edging row 2 and every alt row: Moss st 3, P8, moss st 4.
Edging row 3: Moss st 4, C4B, C4F, moss st 3.
Edging row 5: Moss st 4, K8, moss st 3.
Edging row 6: Moss st 3, P8, moss st 4.
Rep these 6 rows until edging fits around base of sleeve hem.
Cast off sts, decreasing 3 sts across cable.
Stitch into place using mattress stitch or back stitch if preferred.
Join side and sleeve seams.
Place center of cast-off edge of sleeve to shoulder seam. Set in sleeve, easing sleevehead into armhole.

Make button loop
Use 1 strand of yarn and make a 6 cm (**2½ in**) length of chain cording —with a slip knot in right hand, *pull yarn through to make a new slip knot, rep from * until chain is the reqired length. This takes a little practice to get an even tension.
Sew button loop into place at start of neck shaping on right front.
Sew on button to correspond with button loop. 〜

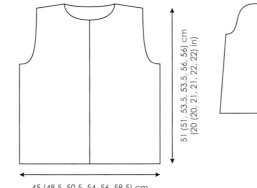

45 (48.5, 50.5, 54, 56, 58.5) cm
(17¾ (19, 20, 20¼, 22, 23) in)

51 (51, 53.5, 53.5, 56, 56) cm
(20 (20, 21, 21, 22, 22) in)

35.5 (35.5, 38, 38, 40.5, 40.5) cm
(14 (14, 15, 15, 16, 16) in)

FRITILLARY

Photographed in early morning on the beach in Portugal, new daylight enhances this simple summer cardigan.
The addition of the edging around the hem and the sleeves makes the garment look far more complex to achieve
than it actually is. The edging does all the work, and the addition of the eyelet band with a twisted cord
threaded through gives the garment shape and definition. Shown in two different lengths and yarn types,
this sweater proves itself to be a truly versatile piece.

To fit dress size:

8	10	12	14	16	18	**US**
10	12	14	16	18	20	**UK**
38	40	42	44	46	48	**EU**

Actual size: Ease allowance approx 10 cm (4 in)

92	98	102	108	112	118	cm
36 ¼	38½	40¼	42½	44	46½	in

Short finished length:

72.5	72.5	72.5	72.5	72.5	72.5	cm
28 ½	28 ½	28 ½	28 ½	28 ½	28 ½	in

Long finished length:

85	85	85	85	85	85	cm
33½	33½	33½	33½	33½	33½	in

Sleeve length:

25.5	25.5	25.5	25.5	25.5	25.5	cm
10	10	10	10	10	10	in

Yarn
Knitted in worsted-weight yarn
Short cardigan
2nd size photographed in Nautical Cotton sh. 23 Sage

13	13	14	14	15	16	x 50g balls

Long cardigan
2nd size photographed in Cinnabar sh. 6 Bluze

14	15	16	16	17	18	x 50g balls

Needles
Pair of 4 mm (US 6) knitting needles
Pair of 4.5 mm (US 7) knitting needles

Button
8 [10] small mother of pearl

Tension/gauge
20 sts x 26 rows to 10cm /4in square measured over
st st using 4.5 mm (US 7) knitting needles

Note
Instructions are for short cardigan first with long version in
[square brackets].

BACK

Using 4 mm (US 6) needles cast on 92(98, 102, 108, 112, 118) sts.
Work 2 rows in garter st.
Change to 4.5 mm (US 7) needles and beg with a K row work 4.5 [17] cm (1¾ [6¾] in) st st, ending with **WS** facing for next row.

BELT EYELETS
Next row (WS): Knit.
Next row: Knit.
Next row: P1, (yo, P2tog) to last st, P1.
Next row: Knit.
Next row: Knit.
Cont to work in st st only until work measures 34.5(34.5, 33.5, 33.5, 32.5, 32.5)cm **(13½, 13½, 13¼, 13¼, 12½, 12½)in)**, [47[47, 46, 46, 45, 45]cm **[18½, 18½, 18, 18, 17¾, 17¾]in]** from cast-on edge, ending with RS facing for next row.

SHAPE ARMHOLES
Cast off 3(5, 6, 7, 8, 9) sts at beg next 2 rows and 3(3, 3, 4, 4, 5) sts at beg 2 foll rows. (80(82, 84, 86, 88, 90) sts)
Dec 1 st at each end of next 3 rows and 3 foll alt rows. (68(70, 72, 74, 76, 78) sts)
Work without further shaping until work measures 18(18, 19, 19, 20, 20)cm **(7(7, 7½, 7½, 8, 8)in)** from armhole, ending with RS facing for next row.

SHAPE SHOULDERS AND BACK NECK
Cast off 4(4, 5, 5, 5, 6) sts at beg next 2 rows.
Cast off 4(4, 5, 5, 5, 6) sts, K until 7(8, 7, 8, 9, 8) sts on needle, turn, leave rem sts on a holder.
Cast off 3 sts, P to end.
Cast off rem 4(5, 4, 5, 6, 5) sts.
Rejoin yarn to rem sts, cast off center 38 sts, K to end.
Complete to match first side, reversing shapings.

LEFT FRONT

Using 4 mm (US 6) needles cast on 46(49, 51, 54, 56, 59) sts.
Work 2 rows in garter st.
Change to 4.5 mm (US 7) needles and beg with a K row work 4.5 [17] cm (1¾ [6¾] in) st st, ending with **WS** facing for next row.

BELT EYELETS
Next row (WS): Knit.
Next row: Knit.
Next row: P1, (yo, P2tog) to last 1(0, 0, 1, 1, 0) st, P1.
Next row: Knit.
Next row: Knit.
Cont to work in st st only until work measures 34.5(34.5, 33.5, 33.5, 32.5, 32.5)cm **(13½, 13½, 13¼, 13¼, 12½, 12½) in)**, [47[47, 46, 46, 45, 45]cm **[18½, 18½, 18, 18, 17¾, 17¾] in]** from cast-on edge, ending with RS facing for next row.

SHAPE ARMHOLE
Cast off 3(5, 6, 7, 8, 9) sts at beg next row and 3(3, 3, 4, 4, 5) sts at beg foll alt row. (40(41, 42, 43, 44, 45) sts)
Work 1 row.
Dec 1 st at armhole edge on next 3 rows and 3 foll alt rows. (34(35, 36, 37, 38, 39) sts)
Work until front is 13 rows shorter than back to shoulder, ending with **WS** facing for next row.

FRONT NECK SHAPING
Cast off 14 sts beg next row and 3 sts at beg foll alt row. (17(18, 19, 20, 21, 22) sts)
Dec 1 st at neck edge on next 3 rows and 2 foll alt rows. (12(13, 14, 15, 16, 17) sts)
Work without further shaping until front matches back to shoulder, ending with RS facing for next row.

SHAPE SHOULDER
Cast off 4(4, 5, 5, 5, 6) sts at beg next row and foll alt row.
Work 1 row.
Cast off rem 4(5, 4, 5, 6, 5) sts.

RIGHT FRONT

Using 4 mm (US 6) needles cast on 46(49, 51, 54, 56, 59) sts.
Work 2 rows in garter st.
Change to 4.5 mm (US 7) needles and beg with a K row work 4.5 [17] cm (1¾ [6¾] in) st st, ending with **WS** facing for next row.

BELT EYELETS
Next row (WS): Knit.
Next row: Knit.
Next row: P1, (yo, P2tog) to last 1(0, 0, 1, 1, 0) st, P1.
Next row: Knit.
Next row: Knit.
Cont to work as for left front, reversing shapings and working an extra row before beg armhole, neck, and shoulder shaping.

SLEEVES (work both the same)

Using 4 mm (US 6) needles cast on 54(54, 58, 58, 62, 62) sts.
Work 2 rows in garter st.
Change to 4.5 mm (US 7) needles and beg with a K row work 8 rows in st st, ending with RS facing for next row.
Inc 1 st at each end next row and 2 foll 10th rows. (60(60, 64, 64, 68, 68) sts)
Cont to work without further shaping until work measures 15.5 cm **(6 in)** from cast on edge, ending with RS facing for next row.

SHAPE SLEEVEHEAD
Cast off 5(5, 6, 6, 7, 7) sts at beg next 2 rows. (50(50, 52, 52, 54, 54) sts)
Dec 1 st at each end of next 3 rows and 4 foll alt rows.

(36(36, 38, 38, 40, 40) sts)
Work 3 rows.
Dec1 st at each end of next row and 2 foll 4th rows.
(30(30, 32, 32, 34, 34) sts)
Work 1 row.
Dec 1 st at each end of next row and 2 foll alt rows,
then on next row. (22(22, 24, 24, 26, 26) sts)
Cast off 3 sts beg next 4 rows.
Cast off rem 10(10, 12, 12, 14, 14) sts.

MAKING UP

Press/block as described in finishing techniques (pg 158).
Join both shoulder seams and side seams using
back stitch.

CARDIGAN EDGING
Using 4.5 mm (US 7) needles cast on 31 sts.
Foundation row: Knit.
Work 20 row patt rep from chart for cardigan edging
setting sts as follows:
Row 1 (RS): K3, yo, k2tog, K1, (yo, K2tog tbl) twice, K1,
(K2tog, yo) twice, K3, yo, K2tog, K5, yo, K2tog, yo, K4.
(32 sts)
Row 2: K2, yo, K2tog, P8, K2, yo, K2tog, P11, K2, yo,
K2tog, K1.
Row 3: K3, yo, K2tog, K2, yo, K2tog tbl, yo, sl1, k2tog, psso,
yo, K2tog, yo, K4, yo, K2tog, K4, (yo, K2tog) twice, yo, K4.
(33 sts)
Row 4: Work picot (cast on 2 sts, cast off 2 sts) (1 st on
RH needle), K1, yo, K2tog, P9, K2, yo, k2tog, P11, K2, yo,
K2tog, K1. (33 sts)
Rep 20 row cardigan edging patt from chart until
edging fits around bottom edge of cardigan starting
at right front edge, across back and along bottom edge
of left front.
Stitch into place.

SLEEVE EDGING (work both the same)
Using 4.5 mm (US 7) needles cast on 16 sts.
Foundation row: Knit.
Work 20 row patt rep from chart for sleeve edging setting
sts as follows:
Row 1 (RS): K3, yo, k2tog, K5, yo, K2tog, yo, K4. (17 sts)
Row 2: K2, yo, K2tog, P8, K2, yo, K2tog, K1.
Row 3: K3, yo, k2tog, K4, (yo, K2tog) twice, yo, K4. (18 sts)
Row 4: Work picot (cast on 2 sts, cast off 2 sts) (1 st on RH
needle), K1, yo, K2tog, P9, K2, yo, K2tog, K1.
Rep 20 row sleeve edging patt from chart until
edging fits around bottom edge of sleeve starting at
underarm seam.
Stitch into place.

BUTTONHOLE BAND
With RS facing of right front and using 4 mm (US 6)
needles, pick up and K 30 sts from lace edging and 98
[130] sts up to right front to neck. (128 [160] sts)

Next row (WS): Knit.
Next row (RS)(buttonholes): K16, *yo, K2tog, K14, rep
from * to end.
Work 2 rows in garter st.
Cast off in Kwise on **WS**.

BUTTONBAND
With RS facing of left front and using 4 mm (US 6)
needles pick up 98 [130] sts down left front to edging
and 30 sts across lace edging. (128 [160] sts)
Work 4 rows in garter st.
Cast off in Kwise on **WS**.

NECK BAND
With RS of right front facing and using 4 mm (US 6)
needles, pick up and K 3 sts from front band, 28 sts up
right front neck to shoulder, 44 sts across back neck and
28 sts down left front neck, and 3 sts from front band.
(106 sts)
Work 2 rows in garter st.
Work picot cast-off as folls:
Cast off 3 sts, *slip st on RH needle back onto LH needle,
cast on 2 sts, then cast off 5 sts, rep from * to end.
Join sleeve seams.
Place center of cast-off edge of sleeve to shoulder
seam. Set in sleeve, easing sleevehead into armhole.
Sew on buttons to correspond with buttonholes and
using picot cast-off as top buttonhole.

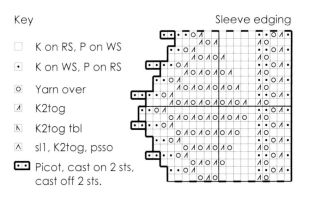

Key

☐   K on RS, P on WS

•   K on WS, P on RS

◦   Yarn over

⟋   K2tog

⟍   K2tog tbl

⋀   sl1, K2tog, psso

▭   Picot, cast on 2 sts,
cast off 2 sts.

Sleeve edging

Cardigan edging

Twisted cord belt

Twisted cord is made as folls: Cut 4 x 4.5-meter **(15 feet)** lengths of yarn. Knot the strands together at each end. Attach one end to a hook or door handle, insert a knitting needle through the other end. Twist the needle—the tighter the twisting, the firmer the finished cord will be. Hold the cord in the center with one hand (you may need some help); bring both ends of cord together, allowing the two halves to twist together. Keep the cord straight and avoid tangling. Knot the cut ends together and trim. This will make a belt approx 1.5 meters **(5 feet)** long.

Starting at center front, thread cord in and out of eyelet holes around center of cardigan as in photograph, knot ends, leaving long lengths as tassels. ∽

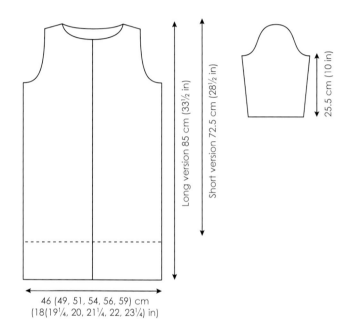

Long version 85 cm (33½ in)

Short version 72.5 cm (28½ in)

25.5 cm (10 in)

46 (49, 51, 54, 56, 59) cm
(18(19¼, 20, 21¼, 22, 23¼) in)

AUGUSTINE

A very simple idea explored in two different ways: I have photographed the garment with a simple one-button neck fastening and a second time with a ribbon threaded through the eyelet border, tied in a pretty feminine bow. The instructions are very simple to follow and the yarn used is bulky-weight so this is a quick knit. The interest comes with the edging, knitted to the main body in a contrasting-weight yarn in a solid shade from the variegated used. The styling of these pictures takes inspiration found in the costumes and coiffure of Marie Antoinette.

TO FIT DRESS SIZE:

8	10	12	14	16	18	**US**
10	12	14	16	18	20	**UK**
38	40	42	44	46	48	**EU**

ACTUAL SIZE: Ease allowance approx 5 cm (2 in)

88	91	97	100	106	109	cm
34½	36	38	39½	42	43	in

FINISHED LENGTH:

43	43	45.5	45.5	48	48	cm
17	17	18	18	19	19	in

SLEEVE LENGTH:

33	33	35.5	35.5	38	38	cm
13	13	14	14	15	15	in

YARN

Knitted in bulky-weight yarn
Jacket with Ribbons
2nd size photographed using Thalia and Kimono Ribbon Pure
A. Thalia sh 8. Beauty

6	6	7	7	8	8	x 50g hanks

B. Kimono Ribbon Pure sh 13. Silver

2	2	2	2	2	2	x 50g balls

Jacket with Button
2nd size photographed using Sari Ribbon and Kimono Ribbon Pure
A. Sari Ribbon sh. 22 Sante

7	7	8	8	9	9	x 50g hanks

B. Kimono Ribbon Pure sh 9 Nut

2	2	2	2	2	2	x 50g balls

NEEDLES

Pair of 6 mm (US 10) knitting needles
Pair of 7 mm (US 10½) knitting needles
Pair of 8 mm (US 11) knitting needles

EXTRAS

Jacket with Ribbons
3 meters (118 ½ in) x 1.3 cm (½ in) ribbon
Jacket with Button
1 large mother of pearl

TENSION/GAUGE

13 sts x 14 rows to 10 cm (4 in) square measured over st st using 8 mm (US 11) needles.

Back

Using 8 mm (US 11) needles and yarn A cast on 57(59, 63, 65, 69, 71) sts.
Work eyelet edging as folls:
Work 3 rows in garter st.
Next row (WS): P1, (yo, P2tog) to end.
Work 2 rows in garter st, ending with RS facing for next row.
Beg with a K row work in st st only until work measures 18(18, 19.5, 19.5, 21, 21) cm **(7(7, 7¾, 7¾, 8¼, 8¼)in)** from cast-on edge, ending with RS facing for next row.

Shape armholes
Cast off 3 sts at beg of next 2 rows and 3 sts at beg of 2 foll rows. (45(47, 51, 53, 57, 59) sts)
Next row (RS) (dec): K3, K2tog, K to last 5 sts, K2tog tbl, K3. (43(45, 49, 51, 55, 57) sts)
Next row: Purl.
Dec 1 st internally as above at each end of next row and 0(0, 1, 2, 3, 3) foll alt rows. (41(43, 45, 45, 47, 49) sts)
Cont without further shaping until armhole measures 18(18, 19, 19, 20, 20) cm **(7(7, 7½, 7½, 8, 8)in)**, ending with RS facing for next row.

Shape shoulders and back neck
Cast off 3(3, 4, 4, 4, 4) sts at beg of next 2 rows.
Next row: Cast off 3(3, 4, 4, 4, 4) sts, K until there are 6(7, 6, 6, 7, 8) sts on RH needle, turn, leave rem sts on a holder for back neck and left shoulder.
Next row: Cast off 3 sts, P to end.
Cast off rem 3(4, 3, 3, 4, 5) sts.
With RS facing, slip center 17 sts onto a holder for back neck, rejoin yarn to rem sts, K to end.
Complete to match first side, reversing shapings.

Left front

Using 8 mm (US 11) needles and yarn A cast on 29(30, 32, 33, 35, 36) sts.
Work eyelet edging as folls:
Work 3 rows in garter st.
Next row (WS): P1, (yo, P2tog) to last 0(1, 1, 0, 0, 1) st, P0(1, 1, 0, 0, 1).
Work 2 rows in garter st, ending with RS facing for next row.
Beg with a K row work in st st only until work measures 18(18, 19.5, 19.5, 21, 21) cm **(7(7, 7¾, 7¾, 8¼, 8¼)in)** from cast on edge, ending with RS facing for next row.

Shape armhole
Cast off 3 sts at beg of next row and 3 sts at beg of foll alt row. (23(24, 26, 27, 29, 30) sts)
Next row: Purl.
Next row (RS) (dec): K3, K2tog, K to end. (22(23, 25, 26, 28, 29) sts)
Next row: Purl.

Dec 1 st internally as above at beg of next row and 0(0, 1, 2, 3, 3) foll alt rows. (21(22, 23, 23, 24, 25) sts)
Work without further shaping until work is 9 rows shorter than back to start of shoulder shaping, ending with **WS** facing for next row.

Shape front neck
Next row (WS): Cast off 8 sts at beg of next row, P to end. (13(14, 15, 15, 16, 17) sts)
Dec 1 st at neck edge on next row and 3 foll rows. (9(10, 11, 11, 12, 13) sts)
Work straight until front matches back to shoulder, ending with RS facing for next row.

Shape shoulder
Cast off 3(3, 4, 4, 4, 4) sts at beg of next row and foll alt row.
Next row: Purl.
Cast off rem 3(4, 3, 3, 4, 5) sts.

Right front

Using 8 mm (US 11) needles and yarn A cast on 29(30, 32, 33, 35, 36) sts.
Work eyelet edging as folls:
Work 3 rows in garter st.
Next row (WS): P1, (yo, P2tog) to last 0(1, 1, 0, 0, 1) st, P0(1, 1, 0, 0, 1).
Work 2 rows in garter st, ending with RS facing for next row.
Beg with a K row work in st st only until work measures 18(18, 19.5, 19.5, 21, 21) cm **(7(7, 7¾, 7¾, 8¼, 8¼)in)** from cast-on edge, ending with **WS** facing for next row.

Shape armhole
Cast off 3 sts at beg of next row and 3 sts at beg of foll alt row. (23(24, 26, 27, 29, 30) sts)
Next row (RS) (dec): K to last 5 sts, K2tog tbl. (22(23, 25, 26, 28, 29) sts)
Next row: Purl.
Dec 1 st internally as above at beg of next row and 0(0, 1, 2, 3, 3) foll alt rows. (21(22, 23, 23, 24, 25) sts)
Work without further shaping until work is 10 rows shorter than back to start of armhole shaping, ending with RS facing for next row.

Shape front neck
Next row (RS): Cast off 8 sts at beg of next row, K to end. (13(14, 15, 15, 16, 17) sts)
Dec 1 st at neck edge on next row and 3 foll rows. (9(10, 11, 11, 12, 13) sts)
Work straight until front matches back to shoulder, ending with **WS** facing for next row.

Shape shoulder
Cast off 3(3, 4, 4, 4, 4) sts at beg of next row and foll alt row.
Next row: Knit.
Cast off rem 3(4, 3, 3, 4, 5) sts.

Sleeves (work both the same)

Using 8 mm (US 11) needles and yarn A cast on 39(39, 41, 41, 43, 43) sts.
Work eyelet edging as folls:
Work 3 rows in garter st.
Next row (WS): P1, (yo, P2tog) to end.
Work 2 rows in garter st, ending with RS facing for next row.
Beg with a K row cont to work in st st only until work measures 26(26, 28.5, 28.5, 31, 31) cm
(10¼(10¼, 11¼, 11¼, 12¼, 12¼)in) from cast-on edge, ending with RS facing for next row.

Shape sleeve head
Cast off 3 sts at beg of next 2 rows.
(33(33, 35, 35, 37, 37) sts)
Dec 1 st at each end of next 3 rows and 8 foll alt rows.
(11(11, 13, 13, 15, 15) sts)
Work 1 row.
Cast off 3 sts beg of next 2 rows.
Cast off rem 5(5, 7, 7, 9, 9) sts.

Making up

Press/block as described in finishing techniques (pg 158).
Join both shoulder seams and side seams using back stitch.

Right front edging
With RS of right front facing and using 7 mm (US 10½) needles and yarn A, pick up and K 38(38, 42, 42, 46, 46) sts from cast-on edge to start of neck shaping.
Work 2 rows in garter st.
Cast off Kwise on **WS**.

Left front edging
With RS of left front facing and using 7 mm (US 10½) needles and yarn A, pick up and knit 38(38, 42, 42, 46, 46) sts from start of neck shaping to cast on edge.
Work 2 rows in garter st.
Cast off Kwise on **WS**.

Neckband
With RS of right front facing and using 7 mm (US 10½) needles and yarn A, pick up and knit 19 sts to shoulder, 3 sts to holder for back neck, K across 17 sts on holder, pick up and knit 3 sts to shoulder and 19 sts down left front. (61 sts)
Jacket with ribbons
Work 2 rows in garter st.
Cast off Kwise on **WS**.
Jacket with button
Next row (WS) (buttonhole): K to last 4 sts, K2tog, yo, K2.
Next row: Knit.
Cast off Kwise on **WS**.

Cardigan edging

Using 6 mm (US 10) needles and yarn B cast on 12 sts.
Work 2 rows in garter st.
Row 1 (RS): K3, yo, K2tog, K1, K2tog, (yo) twice, K2tog, (yo) twice, K2. (14 sts)
Row 2: K3, P1, K2, P1, K4, yo, K2tog, K1.
Row 3: K3, yo, K2tog, K1, K2tog, (yo) twice, K2tog, K4.
Row 4: Cast off 2 sts, K3 (4 sts on needle), P1, K4, yo, K2tog, K1. (12 sts)
Rep these 4 rows until lace edging fits around bottom edge of cardigan starting at right front, across back to left front, ending with RS facing for next row.
Work 3 rows in garter st.
Cast off Kwise on **WS**.
Slip stitch into place.

Sleeve edging (work both the same)
Using 6 mm (US 10) needles and yarn B cast on 12 sts.
Foundation row: Knit.
Row 1 (RS): K3, yo, K2tog, K1, K2tog, (yo) twice, K2tog, (yo) twice, K2. (14 sts)
Row 2: K3, P1, K2, P1, K4, yo, K2tog, K1.
Row 3: K3, yo, K2tog, K1, K2tog, (yo) twice, K2tog, K4.
Row 4: Cast off 2 sts, K3 (4 sts on needle), P1, K4, yo, K2tog, K1. (12 sts)
Rep these 4 rows until lace edging fits around bottom edge of sleeve starting at underarm seam, ending with RS facing for next row.
Cast off.
Slip stitch into place.
Join sleeve seams.
Place center of cast-off edge of sleeves to shoulder seams. Set in sleeves, easing sleevehead into armhole.

Finishing
Jacket with Ribbons
Using photograph as a guide, insert ribbons as follows:
Cut 2 x 1 meter (39½ in) lengths of yarn B, starting at right front opening thread ribbon through eyelet patt, thread across back and left front to left front opening.
Cut 2 x 50 cm (19¾ in) lengths of yarn B, starting at center of sleeve, thread ribbon through eyelet patt on sleeve bringing it back to the start. Tie in a bow.
Repeat for the opposite side.
Jacket with Button
Sew on button to correspond with buttonhole.

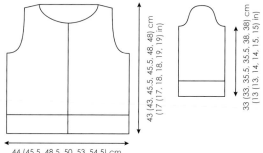

44 (45.5, 48.5, 50, 53, 54.5) cm
(17¼ (18, 19, 19¾, 21, 21½) in)

43 (43, 45.5, 45.5, 48, 48) cm
(17 (17, 18, 18, 19, 19) in)

33 (33, 35.5, 35.5, 38, 38) cm
(13 (13, 14, 14, 15, 15) in)

MINNIE

This design, taken from my Summer Classics collection, has been given different looks by changing up the yarns and adding a lace or cable edging. This is such a versatile piece, and the pattern instructions enable the knitter to choose her own options—long or short sleeves, cable or lace edging. The version made with a wool-silk blend yarn shows how the garment works equally well for winter wear.

TO FIT DRESS SIZE:

8	10	12	14	16	18	**US**
10	12	14	16	18	20	**UK**
38	40	42	44	46	48	**EU**

ACTUAL SIZE: Ease allowance approx 5 cm (2 in)

87	91	97	103	107	111	cm
34¼	36	38	40½	42	43¾	in

FINISHED LENGTH:

40.5	40.5	43	43	45.5	45.5	cm
16	16	17	17	18	18	in

THREE-QUARTER-SLEEVE LENGTH:

30.5	30.5	30.5	30.5	30.5	30.5	cm
12	12	12	12	12	12	in

SHORT SLEEVE LENGTH:

10	10	10	10	10	10	cm
4	4	4	4	4	4	in

YARN
Knitted in worsted-weight yarn
Three-quarter-sleeve cable-edge bolero
1st size photographed in Nautical Cotton sh. 27 Vanilla

9	9	10	10	11	12	x 50g balls

Short-sleeve lace-edge bolero
3rd size photographed in Cinnabar sh. 10 Lilac

8	8	9	9	10	10	x 50g balls

Short-sleeve lace-edge bolero
1st size photographed in Grace Hand Dyed sh. 2 Ice

5	6	6	7	7	8	x 50g hanks

NEEDLES
Pair of 4.5 mm (US 7) knitting needles
Cable needle (cable edge bolero only)

BUTTONS
1 medium mother of pearl

TENSION/GAUGE
Cinnabar
20 sts x 26 rows to 10 cm (4 in) square measured over st st using 4.5 mm (US 7) knitting needles.
Nautical Cotton and Grace
20 sts x 28 rows to 10 cm (4 in) square measured over st st using 4.5 mm (US 7) knitting needles.

Back

Using 4.5 mm (US 7) needles cast on 79(83, 89, 95, 99, 103) sts.
Beg with a K row work 8 rows in st st.
Next row (RS) (inc): K3, M1, K to last 3 sts, M1, K3.
(81(85, 91, 97, 101, 105) sts)
Beg with a P row work 7 rows in st st, ending with RS facing for next row.
Inc 1 st internally at each end as above on next row and 2 foll 8th rows. (87(91, 97, 103, 107, 111) sts)
Cont in st st until work measures 16.5(16.5, 18, 18, 19.5, 19.5) cm **(6½(6½, 7, 7, 7¾, 7¾) in)** from cast-on edge, ending with RS facing for next row.

Shape armholes
Cast off 4(5, 7, 8, 9, 10) sts at beg of next 2 rows and 3(3, 3, 4, 4, 4) sts at beg of 2 foll rows. (73(75, 77, 79, 81, 83) sts)
Next row (RS) (dec): K3, K2tog, K to last 5 sts, K2tog tbl, K3. (71(73, 75, 77, 79, 81) sts)
Next row: Purl.
Dec 1 st internally at each end as above on next row and 2 foll alt rows. (65(67, 69, 71, 73, 75) sts)
Cont without further shaping until armhole measures 18(18, 19, 19, 20, 20) cm **(7(7, 7½, 7½, 8, 8) in)**, ending with RS facing for next row.

Shape shoulders and back neck
Cast off 5(6, 6, 6, 6, 6) sts at beg of next 2 rows.
(55(55, 57, 59, 61, 63) sts)

Shape right shoulder and back neck
Next row (RS): Cast off 5(6, 6, 6, 6, 6) sts, K until there are 9(8, 8, 9, 9, 10) sts on RH needle, turn, leave rem sts on a holder for left shoulder and back neck.
Next row: Cast off 3 sts, P to end.
Cast off rem 6(5, 5, 6, 6, 7) sts.
With RS facing, rejoin yarn to rem sts, cast off center 27(27, 29, 29, 31, 31) sts, K to end.

Shape left shoulder and back neck
Next row (WS): Cast off 5(6, 6, 6, 6, 6) sts, P to end.
Next row: Cast off 3 sts, K to end.
Cast off rem 6(5, 5, 6, 6, 7) sts.

Left front

Using 4.5 mm (US 7) needles cast on 24(26, 29, 32, 34, 36) sts.
Row 1 (RS): Knit.
Row 2 (WS) (inc): Inc into first st, P to end.
Row 3 (inc): K to last st, inc into last st.
Row 4 (inc): Inc into first st, P to end.
(27(29, 32, 35, 37, 39) sts)
Row 5 (inc): K to last st, inc into last st.
(28(30, 33, 36, 38, 40) sts)
Row 6: Purl.
Rep the last 2 rows once more. (29(31, 34, 37, 39, 41) sts)

Row 9 (inc): K3, M1, K to last st, inc into last st.
(31(33, 36, 39, 41, 43) sts)
Row 10: Purl.
Row 11 (inc): K to last st, inc into last st.
(32(34, 37, 40, 42, 44) sts)
Row 12: Purl.
Rep the last 2 rows twice more. (34(36, 39, 42, 44, 46) sts)
Row 17 (inc): K3, M1, K to end. (35(37, 40, 43, 45, 47) sts)
Beg with a P row work 7 rows in st st, ending with RS facing for next row.
Inc 1 st internally at side edge as above on next row and foll 8th row. (37(39, 42, 45, 47, 49) sts)
Cont in st st until work measures 16.5(16.5, 18, 18, 19.5, 19.5) cm **(6½(6½, 7, 7, 7¾, 7¾) in)** from cast-on edge, ending with RS facing for next row.

Shape armhole and front neck
Cast off 4(5, 7, 8, 9, 10) sts at beg of next row and 3(3, 3, 4, 4, 4) sts beg of foll alt row. (30(31, 32, 33, 34, 35) sts)
Work 1 row.
Next row (RS) (dec): K3, K2tog, K to last 5 sts, K2tog tbl, K3. (28(29, 30, 31, 32, 33) sts)
Work 1 row.
Next row (RS) (dec): K3, K2tog, K to end.
(27(28, 29, 30, 31, 32) sts)
Work 1 row.
Rep the last 4 rows once more. (24(25, 26, 27, 28, 29) sts)
Dec 1 st internally at neck edge only as above on next row and 7(7, 8, 8, 9, 9) foll 4th rows.
(16(17, 17, 18, 18, 19) sts)
Cont without further shaping until armhole measures 18(18, 19, 19, 20, 20) cm **(7(7, 7½, 7½, 8, 8) in)**, ending with RS facing for next row.

Shape shoulder
Cast off 5(6, 6, 6, 6, 6) sts at beg of next row and foll alt row.
Work 1 row.
Cast off rem 6(5, 5, 6, 6, 7) sts.

Right front

Using 4.5 mm (US 7) needles cast on 24(26, 29, 32, 34, 36) sts.
Row 1 (RS): Knit.
Row 2 (WS) (inc): P to last st, inc into last st.
Row 3 (inc): Inc into first st, K to end.
Row 4 (inc): P to last st, inc into last st.
(27(29, 32, 35, 37, 39) sts)
Row 5 (inc): Inc into first st, K to end.
(28(30, 33, 36, 38, 40) sts)
Row 6: Purl.
Rep the last 2 rows once more. (29(31, 34, 37, 39, 41) sts)
Row 9 (inc): Inc into first st, K to last 3 sts, M1, K3.
(31(33, 36, 39, 41, 43) sts)
Row 10: Purl.
Row 11 (inc): Inc into first st, K to end.
(32(34, 37, 40, 42, 44) sts)
Row 12: Purl.

Rep the last 2 rows twice more. (34(36, 39, 42, 44, 46) sts)
Row 17 (inc): K to last 3 sts, M1, K3.
(35(37, 40, 43, 45, 47) sts)
Beg with a P row work 7 rows in st st, ending with RS facing for next row.
Inc 1 st internally at side edge as above on next row and foll 8th row. (37(39, 42, 45, 47, 49) sts)
Cont in st st until work measures 16.5(16.5, 18, 18, 19.5, 19.5) cm **(6½(6½, 7, 7, 7¾, 7¾) in)** from cast-on edge, ending with **WS** facing for next row.

SHAPE ARMHOLE AND FRONT NECK
Cast off 4(5, 7, 8, 9, 10) sts at beg of next row and 3(3, 3, 4, 4, 4) sts beg of foll alt row. (30(31, 32, 33, 34, 35) sts)
Next row (RS) (dec): K3, K2tog, K to last 5 sts, K2tog tbl, K3. (28(29, 30, 31, 32, 33) sts)
Work 1 row.
Next row (RS) (dec): K to last 5 sts, K2tog tbl, K3.
(27(28, 29, 30, 31, 32) sts)
Work 1 row.
Rep the last 4 rows once more. (24(25, 26, 27, 28, 29) sts)
Dec 1 st internally at neck edge only as above on next row and 7(7, 8, 8, 9, 9) foll 4th rows.
(16(17, 17, 18, 18, 19) sts)
Cont without further shaping until armhole measures 18(18, 19, 19, 20, 20) cm **(7(7, 7½, 7½, 8, 8) in)**, ending with **WS** facing for next row.

SHAPE SHOULDER
Cast off 5(6, 6, 6, 6, 6) sts at beg of next row and foll alt row.
Work 1 row.
Cast off rem 6(5, 5, 6, 6, 7) sts.

THREE-QUARTER SLEEVES (work both the same)

Using 4.5 mm (US 7) needles cast on 55(55, 59, 59, 63, 63) sts.
Beg with a K row work 14 rows in st st, ending with RS facing for next row.
Next row (RS) (inc): K3, M1, K to last 3 sts, M1, K3.
(57(57, 61, 61, 65, 65) sts)
Beg with a P row work 13 rows in st st, ending with RS facing for next row.
Inc 1 st internally as above at each end of next row and foll 14th row. (61(61, 65, 65, 69, 69) sts)
Cont to work in st st without further shaping until work measures 24.5 cm **(9½ in)** from cast-on edge, ending with RS facing for next row.

SHORT SLEEVES (work both the same)

Using 4.5 mm (US 7) needles cast on 61(61, 65, 65, 69, 69) sts.
Beg with a K row work 10 rows in st st, ending with RS facing for next row.

BOTH SLEEVES

SHAPE SLEEVEHEAD
Cast off 5(5, 6, 6, 7, 7) sts at beg of next 2 rows.
(51(51, 53, 53, 55, 55) sts)
Dec 1 st at each end of next 3 rows and 4 foll alt rows.
(37(37, 39, 39, 41, 41) sts)
Work 3 rows.
Dec 1 st at each end of next row and 2 foll 4th rows.
(31(31, 33, 33, 35, 35) sts)
Work 1 row.
Dec 1 st at each end of next row and 2 foll alt rows, then on next row. (23(23, 25, 25, 27, 27) sts)
Cast off 3 sts beg of next 4 rows.
Cast off rem 11(11, 13, 13, 15, 15) sts.

CABLE EDGE BOLERO

MAKING UP
Press/block as described in finishing techniques (pg 158). Join both shoulder seams and side seams using back stitch.

SLEEVE CABLE EDGING
Using 4.5 mm (US 7) needles cast on 13 sts.
**Cable edging row 1 (RS): K2, yo, K2tog, K7, yo, K2tog.
Cable edging row 2: Cast on 2 sts, cast off 2 sts, (this forms a picot edge), 1 st on RH needle, yo, K2tog, P6, K1, yo, K2tog, K1.
Cable edging row 3: K2, yo, K2tog, K7, yo, K2tog.
Cable edging row 4: K1, yo, K2tog, P6, K1, yo, K2tog, K1.
Cable edging row 5: K2, yo, K2tog, K7, yo, K2tog.
Cable edging row 6: Cast on 2 sts, cast off 2 sts, (this forms a picot edge), 1 st on RH needle, yo, K2tog, P6, K1, yo, K2tog, K1.
Cable edging row 7: K2, yo, K2tog, C6F - slip 3 sts onto cable needle, hold at front, K3, K3 from cable needle, K1, yo, K2tog.
Cable edging row 8: K1, yo, K2tog, P6, K1, yo, K2tog, K1.
These 8 rows form the cable edging patt.**
Rep these 8 rows until cable edging fits around bottom edge of sleeve, ending with **WS** facing for next row.
Cast off Kwise on **WS**.
Slip stitch into place.
Join sleeve seams.
Place center of cast-off edge of sleeves to shoulder seams. Set in sleeves using the set-in method, easing sleeveheads into armholes.

BOLERO CABLE EDGING
Using 4.5 mm (US 7) needles cast on 13 sts.
Work as for sleeve cable edging from ** to **.
Rep these 8 rows until cable edging fits around edging of bolero starting at left hand side seam, up around left front, across back neck, down right front to right hand side seam, and across bottom edge of back, ending with **WS** facing for next row.

Cast off Kwise on **WS**.
Slip stitch into place, allowing ease around front shaping.
Sew on button to left front edging at center front as illustrated in photograph, use eyelet at center front on right front edging as buttonhole.

Lace Edge Bolero

Making up

Press/block as described in finishing techniques (pg 158). Join both shoulder seams and side seams using back stitch.

Sleeve lace edging
Using 4.5 mm (US 7) needles cast on 12 sts.
**Lace edging row 1 (RS): K2, yo, K2tog, yo, K2tog tbl, K1, K2tog, yo, K1, yo, K2tog.
Lace edging row 2: Cast on 2 sts, cast off 2 sts, (this forms a picot edge), 1 st on RH needle, yo, K2tog, P5, K1, yo, K2tog, K1.
Lace edging row 3: K2, yo, K2tog, K1, yo, sl1, K2tog, psso, yo, K2, yo, K2tog.
Lace edging row 4: K1, yo, K2tog, P5, K1, yo, K2tog, K1.
These 4 rows form the lace edging patt.**
Rep these 4 rows until edging fits around bottom edge of sleeve, ending with **WS** facing for next row.
Cast off Kwise on **WS**.
Slip stitch into place.
Join sleeve seams.
Place center of cast-off edge of sleeve to shoulder seam. Set in sleeve, easing sleevehead into armhole.
Sew on buttons to correspond with buttonholes.

Bolero lace edging
Using 4.5 mm (US 7) needles cast on 12 sts.
Work as for sleeve lace edging from ** to **.
Rep these 4 rows until lace edging fits around edging of bolero starting at left hand side seam, up around left front, across back neck, down right front to right hand side seam, and across bottom edge of back, ending with **WS** facing for next row.
Cast off Kwise on **WS**.
Slip stitch into place, allowing ease around front shaping.
Sew on button to left front edging at center front as illustrated in photograph, use eyelet at center front on right front edging as buttonhole.

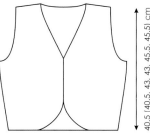

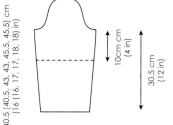

40.5 (40.5, 43, 43, 45.5, 45.5) cm
(16 (16, 17, 17, 18, 18) in)

10cm cm
(4 in)

30.5 cm
(12 in)

43.5 (45.5, 48.5, 51.5, 53.5, 55.5) cm
(17 (18, 19, 20¼, 21, 21¾) in)

Lace, Cables, Fair Isle

In this chapter I explore the idea of adding surface pattern to the cardigan, this is done with the addition of cables, allover lace patterns, and blending color together using the Fair Isle technique. Once again the basic cardigan shapes are very wearable but with the addition of allover pattern they are transformed. You will notice that some designs are shown photographed in different yarns. If you are going to change the yarn, be sure to swatch first. For example, a heavily cabled sweater will look different knitted in a wool-based yarn—the cable will be very springy—versus a cotton based yarn—in which the fabric will be textured and defined. Allover lace patterns are a great way of adding interest to your garment, but take care when shaping armholes and sleeveheads to work only complete pattern repeats, or else you may end up with too many or too few stitches. Fair Isle is a great technique to master, and the two projects in this chapter are a great way to begin your love affair with it.

SILVER

Originally this simple, allover lace cardigan was knitted using a silver ribbon yarn, which gave the garment a very dramatic feel. I wanted to show the versatility of this design so I remade it using a silk-wool blend yarn. As evidenced here, it works extremely well in many different yarns, which transform the definition of the lace stitch.

TO FIT DRESS SIZE:

8	10	12	14	16	18	**US**
10	12	14	16	18	20	**UK**
38	40	42	44	46	48	**EU**

ACTUAL SIZE: Ease allowance approx 7.5 cm (3 in)

89	95	101	107	113	119	cm
35	37½	40	42	44 ½	47	in

FINISHED LENGTH:

40.5	40.5	43	43	45.5	45.5	cm
16	16	17	17	18	18	in

SLEEVE LENGTH:

25.5	25.5	28	28	30.5	30.5	cm
10	10	11	11	12	12	in

YARN

Knitted in worsted-weight yarn
2nd size photographed Louisa Harding in Glisten sh. 2 Silver

9	9	11	11	12	13	x 50g balls

1st size photographed Louisa Harding in Grace Silk & Wool sh. 7 Purple

7	7	8	8	9	9	x 50g balls

NEEDLES

Pair of 4 mm (US 6) knitting needles
Pair of 5 mm (US 8) knitting needles

EXTRAS

1 large button
2 meters (79 in) x 1.3 cm (½ in) ribbon

TENSION/GAUGE

20 sts x 28 rows to 10 cm (4 in) square measured over lace patt using 5 mm (US 8) knitting needles

Back

Using 4 mm (US 6) knitting needles work picot cast-on as folls:
Cast on 5 sts using the cable cast-on method, cast off 2 sts, slip st on RH needle back onto LH needle (3 sts now on LH needle) rep from * to * until 87(93, 99, 105, 111, 117) sts on needle, cast on 2 sts. (89(95, 101, 107, 113, 119) sts)
Work 4 rows in garter st.
Change to 5 mm (US 8) needles and work 8 row lace patt as folls:
Row 1 (RS): Knit.
Row 2 and every WS row: Purl.
Row 3: (K4, K2tog, yo) 14(15, 16, 17, 18, 19) times, K5.
Row 5: Knit.
Row 7: K1, (K2tog, yo, K4) 14(15, 16, 17, 18, 19) times, K2tog, yo, K2.
Row 8: Purl.
Cont to work in lace patt until work measures 22.5(22.5, 24, 24, 25.5, 25.5) cm **(9(9, 9½, 9½, 10, 10)in)** from cast on edge, ending with RS facing for next row.

Shape armholes

Cast off 4(5, 6, 7, 8, 9) sts at beg next 2 rows, and 3(3, 3, 4, 4, 4) sts at beg foll 2 rows. (75(79, 83, 85, 89, 93) sts)
Dec 1 st at armhole edge on next row and 2(3, 4, 4, 4, 4) foll alt rows. (69(71, 73, 75, 79, 83) sts)
Cont without further shaping until armhole measures 18(18, 19, 19, 20, 20) cm **(7(7, 7½, 7½, 8, 8)in)**, ending with RS facing for next row.

Shape shoulders and back neck

Cast off 6(6, 6, 7, 7, 8) sts at beg next 2 rows.
Cast off 6(6, 6, 7, 7, 8) sts at beg next row, patt until 8(9, 10, 9, 11, 11) sts on RH needle, turn, work both sides of neck separately.
Cast off 3 sts, P to end.
Cast off rem 5(6, 7, 6, 8, 8) sts.
Rejoin yarn to rem sts, cast off center 29 sts, patt to end.
Complete to match first side, reversing shapings.

Left front

Using 4 mm (US 6) knitting needles work picot cast-on as folls:
Cast on 5 sts using the cable cast-on method, cast off 2 sts, slip st on RH needle back onto LH needle (3 sts now on LH needle) rep from * to * until 42(45, 48, 51, 54, 57) sts on needle, cast on 2 sts. (44(47, 50, 53, 56, 59) sts)
Work 4 rows in garter st.
Change to 5 mm (US 8) needles and work 8 row lace patt as folls:
Row 1 (RS): Knit.
Row 2 and every WS row: Purl.
Row 3: (K4, K2tog, yo) 7(7, 8, 8, 9, 9) times, K2(5, 2, 5, 2, 5).
Row 5: Knit.
Row 7: K1, (K2tog, yo, K4) 7(7, 8, 8, 9, 9) times, K1(4, 1, 4, 1, 4).

Row 8: Purl.
Cont to work in lace patt until work measures 22.5(22.5, 24, 24, 25.5, 25.5) cm **(9(9, 9½, 9½, 10, 10)in)** from cast-on edge, ending with RS facing for next row.

Shape armhole

Cast off 4(5, 6, 7, 8, 9) sts at beg next row, and 3(3, 3, 4, 4, 4) sts at beg foll alt row. (37(39, 41, 42, 44, 46) sts)
Work 1 row.
Dec 1 st at armhole edge on next row and 2(3, 4, 4, 4, 4) foll alt rows. (34(35, 36, 37, 39, 41) sts)
Work in patt without further shaping until front is 15 rows shorter than back to shoulder shaping, ending with **WS** facing for next row.

Shape front neck

Cast off 9 sts at beg next row and 3 sts beg foll alt row. (22(23, 24, 25, 27, 29) sts)
Dec 1 st at neck edge on next 2 rows and 3 foll alt rows. (17(18, 19, 20, 22, 24) sts)
Work until front matches back to shoulder, ending with RS facing for next row.

Shape shoulder

Cast off 6(6, 6, 7, 7, 8) sts beg next row and foll alt row.
Work 1 row.
Cast off rem 5(6, 7, 6, 8, 8) sts.

Right front

Using 4 mm (US 6) knitting needles work picot cast-on as folls:
Cast on 5 sts using the cable cast on method, cast off 2 sts, slip st on RH needle back onto LH needle (3 sts now on LH needle) rep from * to * until 42(45, 48, 51, 54, 57) sts on needle, cast on 2 sts. (44(47, 50, 53, 56, 59) sts)
Work 4 rows in garter st.
Change to 5 mm (US 8) needles and work 8 row lace patt as folls:
Row 1 (RS): Knit.
Row 2 and every WS row: Purl.
Row 3: K1(4, 1, 4, 1, 4), (K2tog, yo, K4) 7(7, 8, 8, 9, 9) times, K1.
Row 5: Knit.
Row 7: K4(7, 4, 7, 4, 7), (K2tog, yo, K4) 6(6, 7, 7, 8, 8) times, K2tog, yo, K2.
Row 8: Purl.
Cont to work in lace patt until work measures 22.5(22.5, 24, 24, 25.5, 25.5) cm **(9(9, 9½, 9½, 10, 10)in)** from cast-on edge, ending with **WS** facing for next row.
Complete to match left front, reversing shapings and working an extra row before beg armhole, neck, and shoulder shaping.

SLEEVES (work both the same)

Using 4 mm (US 6) knitting needles work picot cast-on as folls:
Cast on 5 sts using the cable cast-on method, cast off 2 sts, slip st on RH needle back onto LH needle (3 sts now on LH needle) rep from * to * until 54(54, 57, 57, 57, 57) sts on needle, cast on 1(1, 0, 0, 2, 2) sts.
(55(55, 57, 57, 59, 59)sts)
Work 4 rows in garter st.
Change to 5 mm (US 8) needles and work 8 row lace patt as folls:
Row 1 (RS): Knit.
Row 2 and every WS row: Purl.
Row 3: K2(2, 3, 3, 4, 4), (K2tog, yo, K4) 8 times, K2tog, yo, K3(3, 4, 4, 5, 5).
Row 5: Knit.
Row 7: K5(5, 6, 6, 7, 7), (K2tog, yo, K4) 8 times, K2(2, 3, 3, 4, 4).
Row 8: Purl.
Work 8 rows more in lace patt.
Inc 1 st at each end of next row and every foll 16th(16th, 14th, 14th, 12th, 12th)row to 61(61, 65, 65, 69, 69) sts.
Work without further shaping until work measures 25.5(25.5, 28, 28, 30.5, 30.5) cm **(10(10, 11, 11, 12, 12)in)** from cast-on edge.

SHAPE SLEEVEHEAD

Cast off 5 sts at beg next 2 rows. (51(51, 55, 55, 59, 59) sts)
Dec 1 st at each end of next 3 rows and 3 foll alt rows. (39(39, 43, 43, 47, 47) sts)
Work 3 rows.
Dec 1 st at each end of next row and 3 foll 4th rows. (31(31, 35, 35, 39, 39) sts)
Work 1 row.
Dec 1 st at each end of next row and 3 foll alt rows, then on next row. 21(21, 25, 25, 29, 29) sts.
Cast off 3 sts at beg next 4 rows. (9(9, 13, 13, 17, 17) sts)
Cast off.

MAKING UP

Press/block as described in finishing techniques (pg 158).
Join both shoulder seams.

RIGHT FRONT EDGING

With RS facing and using 4 mm (US 6) needles, starting at bottom edge, pick up and K 69(69, 75, 75, 79, 79) sts up right front edge to neck shaping.
Work 2 rows in garter st.
Work picot cast-off as folls:
Cast off 3 sts, *slip st on RH needle back onto LH needle, cast on 2 sts, then cast off 5 sts, rep from * to end.

LEFT FRONT EDGING

With RS facing and using 4 mm (US 6) needles, starting at neck edge, pick up and K 69(69, 75, 75, 79, 79) sts down left front edge to end.
Work 2 rows in garter st.
Work picot cast-off as for right front edging.

NECKBAND

With RS of right front facing and using 4 mm (US 6) needles, pick up and K 3 sts from front band and 27 sts up right front neck to shoulder, 35 sts across back neck and 27 sts down left front neck, and 3 sts from front band. (95 sts)
Work 2 rows in garter st.
Work picot cast-off as for right front edging.
Join side and sleeve seams.
Place center of cast-off edge of sleeve to shoulder seam. Set in sleeve, easing sleevehead into armhole.
Make a button loop: Use 1 strand of yarn A and make 1 x 6.5 cm **(2½ in)** length of chain cording —with a slip knot in right hand, *pull yarn through to make a new slip knot, rep from * until chain is the reqired length. This takes a little practice to get an even tension. Sew button loop into place at start of neck shaping on right front. Sew button on to left front to correspond with button loop. Alternatively cut length of ribbon into half, secure either side of front neck edge with a few stitches to hold ribbon in place, tie in a bow.

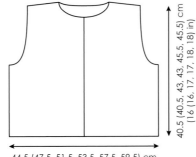

44.5 (47.5, 51.5, 53.5, 57.5, 59.5) cm
(17½ (18¾, 20¼, 21, 22¾, 23½) in)

40.5 (40.5, 43, 43, 45.5, 45.5) cm
(16 (16, 17, 17, 18, 18) in)

25.5 (25.5, 28, 28, 30.5, 30.5) cm
(10 (10, 11, 11, 12, 12) in)

WATERFALL

This design uses two different techniques, Fair Isle for the main body of the cardigan and an open lace stitch for the sleeves. I like to mix different techniques in one design, as it makes a unique and interesting experience for the knitter. The vibrant colors of the Grace silk and wool yarn beautifully blend in this Fair Isle pattern.

TO FIT DRESS SIZE:

8	10	12	14	16	18	**US**
10	12	14	16	18	20	**UK**
38	40	42	44	46	48	**EU**

ACTUAL SIZE: Ease allowance approx 5 cm (2 in)

86	91	96	103	106	109	cm
34	36	37 ¾	40½	41¾	43	in

FINISHED LENGTH:

48.5	48.5	51	51	53.5	53.5	cm
19	19	20	20	21	21	in

SLEEVE LENGTH:

45.5	45.5	48.5	48.5	51	51	cm
18	18	19	19	20	20	in

YARN

Knitted in double knitting–weight yarn
1st size photographed in Louisa Harding Grace
A. sh. 8 Purple

2	2	3	3	3	3	x 50g balls

B. sh. 5 Moss

6	6	7	7	7	8	x 50g balls

C. sh. 4 Powder

2	2	2	2	3	3	x 50g balls

D. sh. 6 Ruby

2	2	2	2	2	2	x 50g balls

E. sh. 7 Peacock

2	2	2	2	2	2	x 50g balls

NEEDLES

Pair of 3.75 mm (US 5) knitting needles
Pair of 4.5 mm (US 7) knitting needles

BUTTON

1 medium mother of pearl

TENSION/GAUGE

Fair Isle pattern
24 sts x 26 rows to 10cm (4 in) square measured over
Fair Isle patt using 4.5 mm (US 7) knitting needles
Lace pattern
19 sts x 28 rows to 10cm (4 in) square measured over
lace patt using 4.5 mm (US 7) knitting needles

Back

Using 3.75 mm (US 5) needles and yarn A cast on 103(109, 115, 123, 127, 131) sts.
Next row (RS): (K1, P1) to last st, K1.
Next row: (K1, P1) to last st, K1.
These 2 rows form moss st.
Work 4 more rows in moss st.
Change to 4.5 mm (US 7) needles and yarn B.
Joining in and breaking off yarn as required rep 34 rows of Fair Isle pattern from chart beg and ending rows as indicated on chart for appropriate size.
Work in patt until work measures 30.5(30.5, 32, 32, 33.5, 33.5)cm **(12(12, 12½, 12½, 13, 13)in)** from cast-on edge, ending with RS facing for next row.

Shape Armholes

Cast off 4(5, 7, 9, 9, 9) sts at beg next 2 rows and 3(3, 3, 4, 4, 4) sts at beg 2 foll rows. (89(93, 95, 97, 101, 105) sts)
Dec 1 st at each end of next 3 rows and 2(3, 3, 3, 3, 3) foll alt rows. (79(81, 83, 85, 89, 93) sts)
Work in patt without further shaping until work measures 18(18, 19, 19, 20, 20) cm **(7(7, 7½, 7½, 8, 8)in)** from armhole, ending with RS facing for next row.

Shape shoulders and back neck

Cast off 6(6, 7, 7, 8, 8) sts at beg next 2 rows.
Cast off 6(6, 7, 7, 8, 8) sts, patt until 9(10, 9, 10, 10, 12) sts remain on needle, turn, leave rem sts on a holder.
Cast off 3 sts, patt to end.
Cast off rem 6(7, 6, 7, 7, 9) sts.
Rejoin yarn to rem sts, cast off center 37 sts, patt to end.
Complete to match first side, reversing shapings.

Left front

Using 3.75 mm (US 5) needles and yarn A cast on 51(53, 57, 61, 63, 65) sts.
Next row (RS): (K1, P1) to last st, K1.
Next row: (K1, P1) to last st, K1.
These 2 rows form moss st.

2nd size only

Work 3 more rows in moss st.
Next row (WS) (inc): Moss st to last st, inc in last st. (54 sts)

1st, 3rd, 4th, 5th & 6th sizes

Work 4 more rows in moss st.

All sizes

Change to 4.5 mm (US 7) needles and yarn B.
Joining in and breaking off yarn as required rep 34 rows of Fair Isle pattern from chart beg and ending rows as indicated on chart for appropriate size.
Work in patt until work measures 30.5(30.5, 32, 32, 33.5, 33.5)cm **(12(12, 12½, 12½, 13, 13)in)** from cast-on edge, ending with RS facing for next row.

Shape armhole

Cast off 4(5, 7, 9, 9, 9) sts at beg next row and 3(3, 3, 4, 4, 4) sts at beg foll alt row. (44(46, 47, 48, 50, 52) sts)
Work 1 row.
Dec 1 st at armhole edge on next 3 rows and 2(3, 3, 3, 3, 3) foll alt rows. (39(40, 41, 42, 44, 46) sts)
Work in patt without further shaping until front is 13 rows shorter than back to shoulder shaping, ending with **WS** for next row.

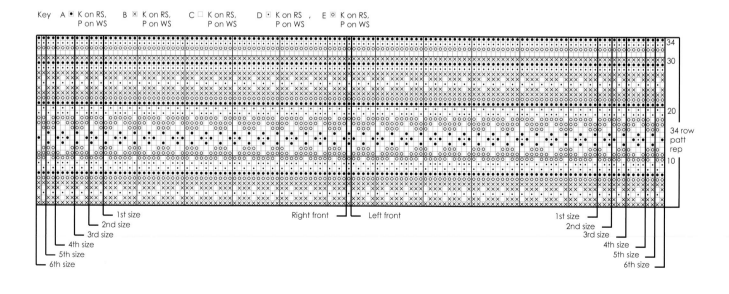

Key A ▪ K on RS,   B ☒ K on RS,   C ☐ K on RS,   D ▫ K on RS ,   E ◉ K on RS,
P on WS   P on WS   P on WS   P on WS   P on WS

Shape front neck
Cast off 13 sts at beg next row and 4 sts at beg foll alt row. (22(23, 24, 25, 27, 29) sts)
Dec 1 st at neck edge on next 4 rows.
(18(19, 20, 21, 23, 25) sts)
Work until front matches back to shoulder, ending with RS facing for next row.

Shape shoulder
Cast off 6(6, 7, 7, 8, 8) sts beg next row and foll alt row.
Work 1 row.
Cast off rem 6(7, 6, 7, 7, 9) sts.

Right front

Using 3.75 mm (US 6) needles and yarn A cast on 51(53, 57, 61, 63, 65) sts.
Next row (RS): (K1, P1) to last st, K1.
Next row: (K1, P1) to last st, K1.
These 2 rows form moss st.

2nd size only
Work 3 more rows in moss st.
Next row (WS) (inc): Inc in first st, moss st to end. (54 sts)

1st, 3rd, 4th, 5th & 6th sizes
Work 4 more rows in moss st.

All sizes
Change to 4.5 mm (US 7) needles and yarn B.
Joining in and breaking off yarn as required rep 34 rows of Fair Isle pattern from chart beg and ending rows as indicated on chart for appropriate size.
Work in patt until work measures 30.5(30.5, 32, 32, 33.5, 33.5)cm **(12(12, 12½, 12½, 13, 13)in)** from cast-on edge, ending with RS facing for next row.
Complete to match left front reversing all shapings

Sleeves (work both the same)

Using 3.75 mm (US 6) needles and yarn B cast on 61 sts.
Next row (RS) (dec): (K1, P1) to last st, K1.
Next row: (K1, P1) to last st, K1.
These 2 rows form moss st.
Work 4 more rows in moss st.
Change to 4.5 mm (US 7) needles and work in 4 row lace patt setting sts as folls:
Row 1 (RS): K1, [(yo, K2tog tbl) twice, K1, (K2tog, yo) twice, K1] 6 times.
Row 2: K1, P to last st, K1.
Row 3: K1, [K1, yo, K2tog tbl, yo, sl1, K2tog, psso, yo, K2tog, yo, K2] 6 times.
Row 4: K1, P to last st, K1.
These 4 rows form lace patt and are rep throughout.

Work without further shaping until work measures 45.5(45.5, 48.5, 48.5, 51, 51) cm **(18(18, 19, 19, 20, 20)in)** from cast-on edge, ending with RS facing for next row.

Shape sleevehead

NOTE:
Do not work any incomplete lace patterns when shaping sleeve head; work incomplete patt reps in st st.

1st & 2nd size
Cast off 5 sts at beg next 2 rows. (51 sts)
Dec 1 st at each end of next 3 rows and 3 foll alt rows. (39 sts)
Work 3 rows.
Dec1 st at each end of next row and 3 foll 4th rows. (31 sts)
Work 1 row.
Dec 1 st at each end of next row and 2 foll alt rows, then every row until 19 sts rem, ending with RS facing for next row.

3rd & 4th size
Cast off 5 sts at beg next 2 rows. (51 sts)
Dec 1 st at each end of next 3 rows and 2 foll alt rows. (41 sts)
Work 3 rows.
Dec1 st at each end of next row and 5 foll 4th rows. (29 sts)
Work 1 row.
Dec 1 st at each end of next row and foll alt row, then every row until 19 sts rem, ending with RS facing for next row.

5th & 6th size
Cast off 5 sts at beg next 2 rows. (51 sts)
Dec 1 st at each end of next 3 rows and 2 foll alt rows. (41 sts)
Work 3 rows.
Dec1 st at each end of next row and foll 4th row. (37 sts)
Work 5 rows.
Dec1 st at each end of next row and foll 6th row. (33 sts)
Work 3 rows.
Dec1 st at each end of next row and foll 4th row. (29 sts)
Work 1 row.
Dec 1 st at each end of next row and foll alt row, then every row until 19 sts rem, ending with RS facing for next row.

All sizes
Cast off 3 sts at beg next 4 rows.
Cast off rem 7 sts.

Making up

Press/block as described in finishing techniques (pg 158).
Join both shoulder seams using back stitch.

Right front band
With RS of right front facing and using 3.75 mm (US 5)
needles and yarn A, pick up and K91(91, 95, 95,
101, 101) sts up right front to neck.
Work 4 rows in moss st as given for back, ending with **WS**
facing for next row.
Cast off Kwise on **WS**.

Left front band
With RS of left front facing and using 3.75 mm (US 5)
needles and yarn A, pick up and K91(91, 95, 95,
101, 101) sts down left front.
Work 4 rows in moss st as given for back, ending with **WS**
facing for next row.
Cast off Kwise on **WS**.

Neck band
With RS of right front facing and using 3.75 mm (US 5)
needles and yarn A, pick up and K 3 sts from front band
and 26 sts up right front neck to shoulder, 43 sts across
back neck and 26 sts down left front neck, and 3 sts from
front band. (101 sts)
Next row (WS): (K1, P1) to last st, K1.
Next row (RS) (buttonhole): K1, K2 tog, yo, patt to end.
Work 2 more rows in moss st.
Cast off Kwise on **WS**.
Join side and sleeve seams.
Place center of cast-off edge of sleeve to shoulder
seam. Set in sleeve, easing sleevehead into armhole.
Sew on button to correspond with buttonhole.

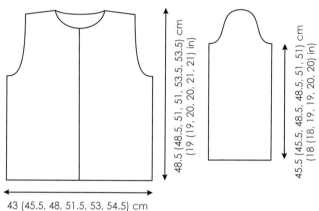

43 (45.5, 48, 51.5, 53, 54.5) cm
(17 (18, 19, 20¼, 21, 21½) in)

48.5 (48.5, 51, 51, 53.5, 53.5) cm
(19 (19, 20, 20, 21, 21) in)

45.5 (45.5, 48.5, 48.5, 51, 51) cm
(18 (18, 19, 19, 20, 20) in)

MASQUERADE

I love the vintage feel of this two-colored Fair Isle cardigan; it is reminiscent of the little cardigans that girls would have worn with their prom dresses in the 1950s. I love the way the Fair Isle fades into small little spots the further up the garment it is worked. This is the perfect project to learn the Fair Isle technique, just remember to weave in the floats on the reverse side loosely, otherwise the fabric will be stiff and pucker.

To fit dress size:

8	10	12	14	16	18	**US**
10	12	14	16	18	20	**UK**
38	40	42	44	46	48	**EU**

Actual size: Ease allowance approx 5 cm (2 in)

86	90	97	103	106	110	cm
34	35½	38¼	40½	41¾	43¼	in

Finished length:

48.5	48.5	51	51	53.5	53.5	cm
19	19	20	20	21	21	in

Sleeve length:

37	37	39.5	39.5	42	42	cm
14 ½	14 ½	15 ½	15 ½	16 ½	16½	in

Yarn

Knitted in double knitting–weight yarn
1st size photographed in Louisa Harding Kimono Angora Pure

A. sh. 8 Soot

2	2	2	2	2	2	x 25g balls

B. sh. 1 Rice

6	6	7	7	8	8	x 25g balls

Needles

Pair of 3.25 mm (US 3) knitting needles
Pair of 4 mm (US 6) knitting needles
Pair of 4.5 mm (US 7) knitting needles

Buttons

7 small mother of pearl

Tension/gauge

22 sts x 30 rows to 10cm (4in) square measured over Fair Isle patt using 4.5 mm (US 7) knitting needles
22 sts x 30 rows to 10cm (4in) square measured over st st using 4 mm (US 6) knitting needles

Back

Using 3.25 mm (US 3) needles and yarn A cast on 94(98, 106, 114, 118, 122) sts.
Change to yarn B and work in rib setting sts as folls:
Next row (RS): (K2, P2) to last 2 sts, K2.
Next row: P2, (K2, P2) to end.
These 2 rows form rib.
Work 13 more rows in rib.
Next row (WS): Inc (inc, inc, dec, dec, dec) 1 st at beg next row, rib to end. (95(99, 107, 113, 117, 121) sts)
Change to 4.5 mm (US 7) needles and, joining in and breaking off yarn as required, work Fair Isle pattern from chart beg and ending rows as indicated on chart for appropriate size to chart row 50.
Change to 4 mm (US 6) needles and work 12 row patt rep from chart.
Cont to rep these 12 rows until work measures 30.5(30.5, 32, 32, 33.5, 33.5)cm **(12(12, 12½, 12½, 13, 13)in)** from cast-on edge, ending with RS facing for next row.

Shape armholes

Cast off 4(5, 7, 8, 9, 10) sts at beg next 2 rows and 3(3, 3, 4, 4, 4) sts at beg 2 foll rows.
(81(83, 87, 89, 91, 93) sts)
Dec 1 st at each end of next row and 3(3, 4, 4, 4, 4) foll alt rows. (73(75, 77, 79, 81, 83) sts)
Work in patt without further shaping until work measures 18(18, 19, 19, 20, 20) cm **(7(7, 7½, 7½, 8, 8)in)** from armhole, ending with RS facing for next row.

Shape shoulders and back neck

Cast off 7(7, 7, 7, 7, 8) sts at beg next 2 rows.
Cast off 7(7, 7, 7, 7, 8) sts, patt until 9(10, 10, 11, 11, 10) sts on needle, turn, leave rem sts on a holder.
Cast off 3 sts, patt to end.
Cast off rem 6(7, 7, 8, 8, 7) sts.
Rejoin yarn to rem sts, cast off center 27(27, 29, 29, 31, 31) sts, patt to end.
Complete to match first side, reversing shapings.

Key   A · K on RS, P on WS   B ☐ K on RS, P on WS

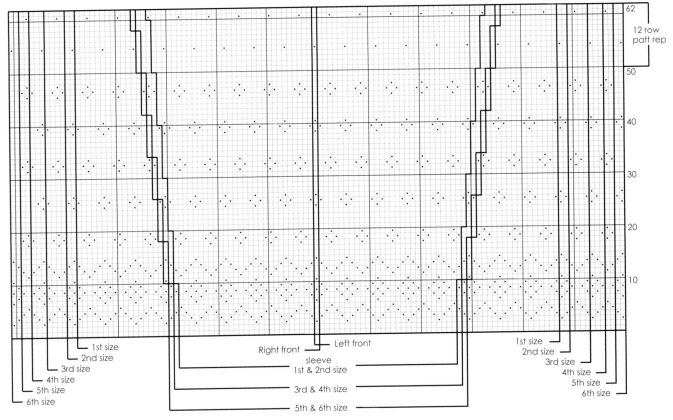

Left front

Using 3.25 mm (US 3) needles and yarn A cast on 50(50, 54, 58, 58, 62) sts.
Change to yarn B and work in rib setting sts as folls:
Next row (RS): (K2, P2) to last 2 sts, K2.
Next row: P2, (K2, P2) to end.
These 2 rows form rib.
Work 13(14, 14, 13, 13, 13) rows in rib.

1st size
Next row (WS): Dec 1 st at beg and end of row. (48 sts)

5th size
Next row (WS): Inc 1 st at end of row. (59 sts)

4th & 6th size
Next row (WS): Dec 1 st at end of row. (57(61) sts)
Change to 4.5 mm (US 7) needles and, joining in and breaking off yarn as required, work Fair Isle pattern from chart beg and ending rows as indicated on chart for appropriate size to chart row 50.
Change to 4 mm (US 6) needles and work 12 row patt rep from chart.
Cont to rep these 12 rows until work measures 30.5(30.5, 32, 32, 33.5, 33.5)cm **(12(12, 12½, 12½, 13, 13)in)** from cast on edge, ending with RS facing for next row.

Shape armhole
Cast off 4(5, 7, 8, 9, 10) sts at beg next row and 3(3, 3, 4, 4, 4) sts at beg foll alt row. (41(42, 44, 45, 46, 47) sts)
Work 1 row.
Dec 1 st at armhole edge on next row and 3(3, 4, 4, 4, 4) foll alt rows. (37(38, 39, 40, 41, 42) sts)
Work in patt without further shaping until work is 11 rows shorter than back to shoulder shaping, ending with **WS** facing for next row.

Shape front neck
Cast off 10(10, 11, 11, 12, 12) sts at beg next row and 3 sts at beg foll alt row. (24(25, 25, 26, 26, 27) sts)
Dec 1 st at neck edge on next 4 rows.
(20(21, 21, 22, 22, 23) sts)
Work until front matches back to shoulder, ending with RS facing for next row.

Shape shoulder
Cast off 7(7, 7, 7, 7, 8) sts beg next row and foll alt row.
Work 1 row.
Cast off rem 6(7, 7, 8, 8, 7) sts.

Right front

Using 3.25 mm (US 3) needles and yarn A cast on 50(50, 54, 58, 58, 62) sts.
Change to yarn B and work in rib setting sts as folls:
Next row (RS): (K2, P2) to last 2 sts, K2.

Next row: P2, (K2, P2) to end.
These 2 rows form rib.
Work 13(14, 14, 13, 13, 13) rows in rib.

1st size
Next row (WS): Dec 1 st at beg and end of row. (48 sts)

5th size
Next row (WS): Inc 1 st at beg of row. (59 sts)

4th & 6th size
Next row (WS): Dec 1 st at beg of row. (57(61) sts)
Change to 4.5 mm (US 7) needles and, joining in and breaking off yarn as required, work Fair Isle pattern from chart beg and ending rows as indicated on chart for appropriate size to chart row 50.
Change to 4 mm (US 6) needles and work 12 row patt rep from chart.
Cont to rep these 12 rows until work measures 30.5(30.5, 32, 32, 33.5, 33.5)cm **(12(12, 12½, 12½, 13, 13)in)** from cast-on edge, ending with **WS** facing for next row.
Complete to match left front, reversing shapings and working an extra row before working armhole, neck, and shoulder shaping.

Sleeves (work both the same)

Using 3.25 mm (US 3) needles and yarn A cast on 54(54, 58, 58, 58, 58) sts.
Change to yarn B and work in rib setting sts as folls:
Next row (RS): (K2, P2) to last 2 sts, K2.
Next row: P2, (K2, P2) to end.
These 2 rows form rib.
Work 13 more rows in rib.
Next row (WS): Inc(inc, dec, dec, inc, inc) 1 st at beg next row, rib to end. (55(55, 57, 57, 59, 59) sts)
Change to 4.5 mm (US 7) needles and, joining in and breaking off yarn as required, work Fair Isle pattern from chart for sleeve beg and ending rows as indicated on chart for appropriate size and increasing 1 st at each end of chart row 11 and every foll 10th(10th, 8th, 8th, 8th, 8th) row to chart row 50.
Change to 4 mm (US 6) needles and cont to work 12 row patt rep from chart keeping side incs correct until there are 71(71, 75, 75, 79, 79) sts.
Work without further shaping until work measures 37(37, 39.5, 39.5, 42, 42)cm **(14½(14½, 15½, 15½, 16½, 16½)in)** from cast-on edge, ending with RS facing for next row.

Shape sleevehead
Cast off 4 sts at beg next 2 rows and 3 sts at beg 2 foll rows. (57(57, 61, 61, 65, 65) sts)
Dec 1 st at each end of next 3 rows and 3 foll alt rows. (45, 45, 49, 49, 53, 53) sts)
Work 3 rows.
Dec 1 st at each end of next row and 2 foll 4th rows. (39(39, 43, 43, 47, 47) sts)

Work 1 row.
Dec 1 st at each end of next row and 4 foll alt rows,
then on every foll row until 23(23, 27, 27, 31, 31) sts rem,
ending with RS facing for next row.
Cast off 3 sts beg next 4 rows.
Cast off rem 11(11, 15, 15, 19, 19) sts.

Making up

Press/block as described in finishing techniques (pg 158).
Join both shoulder seams using back stitch.

Buttonhole band

With RS facing of right front and using 3.25 mm (US 3)
needles and yarn B, pick up and K97(97, 103, 103, 109,
109) sts up right front to neck.
Next row (WS): Knit.
Next row (RS) (buttonholes): K1, (K2tog, yo, K14(14, 15, 15,
16, 16) 6 times.
Next row (WS): Knit.
Cast off Kwise on WS.

Buttonband

With RS of left front facing and using 3.25 mm (US 3)
needles and yarn B, pick up and K97(97, 103, 103,
109, 109) sts down left front.
Work 3 rows in garter st.
Cast off Kwise on **WS**.

Neck band

With RS of right front facing and using 3.25 mm (US 3)
needles and yarn B, pick up and K 3 sts from front band
and 23(23, 26, 26, 29, 29) sts up right front neck
to shoulder, 33(33, 35, 35, 37, 37) sts across back neck
and 23(23, 26, 26, 29, 29) sts down left front neck, and 3
sts from front band. (85(85, 93, 93, 101, 101) sts)
Next row (WS): Knit.
Next row (RS) (buttonhole): K1, K2 tog, yo, K to end.
Next row (WS): Knit.
Cast off Kwise on **WS**.
Join side and sleeve seams.
Place center of cast-off edge of sleeve to shoulder
seam. Set in sleeve, easing sleevehead into armhole.
Sew on buttons to correspond with buttonholes.

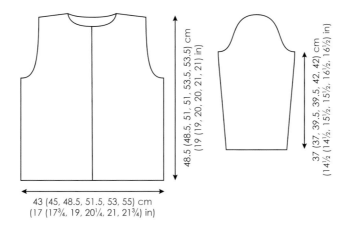

43 (45, 48.5, 51.5, 53, 55) cm
(17 (17¾, 19, 20¼, 21, 21¾) in)

48.5 (48.5, 51, 51, 53.5, 53.5) cm
(19 (19, 20, 20, 21, 21) in)

37 (37, 39.5, 39.5, 42, 42) cm
(14½ (14½, 15½, 15½, 16½, 16½) in)

VERTIGO

This flattering cardigan is worked in a large cable design, with the cables traveling in opposite directions to give the illusion of height to the wearer. The front fastening is a series of loops created when working the front band cast off. Designed to fit where it touches and to enhance and make the most of curves, the twisted cord belt also helps cinch in the waist.

To fit dress size:

8	10	12	14	16	18	**US**
10	12	14	16	18	20	**UK**
38	40	42	44	46	48	**EU**

Actual size: Ease allowance approx 7.5 cm (3 in)

98	104	108	112	118	122	cm
38½	41	42½	44	46½	48	in

Finished length:

71	71	72	72	73	73	cm
28	28	28½	28½	29	29	in

Sleeve length:

45.5	45.5	48.5	48.5	51	51	cm
18	18	19	19	20	20	in

Yarn

Knitted in aran-weight yarn.
2nd size photographed in Louisa Harding Kashmir Aran
sh. 13 Duck Egg

17	18	19	20	21	22	x 50g balls

Needles

Pair of 4.5 mm (US 7) knitting needles
Pair of 5 mm (US 8) knitting needles
Cable needle

Buttons

7 medium mother of pearl

Tension/gauge

20 sts x 24 rows to 10cm (4 in) square measured over cable and rib patt using 5 mm (US 8) knitting needles

Back

Using 4.5 mm (US 7) needles cast on 98(104, 108, 112, 118, 122) sts.
Work 10 rows from body chart beg and ending rows as indicated on chart for appropriate size.
Change to 5 mm (US 8) needles and work 12 rows in cable and rib patt rep from chart.
Rep 12 row cable patt throughout and AT THE SAME TIME dec 1 st either side next row and 4 foll 8th rows.
(88(94, 98, 102, 108, 112) sts)
Cont without any further shaping until work measures 26.5 cm **(10½)in)** from cast-on edge, ending with RS facing for next row.
Inc 1 st at each end of next row and 4 foll 8th rows to 98(104, 108, 112, 118, 122) sts.
Cont without further shaping until work measures 53 cm **(21in)** from cast-on edge, ending with RS facing for next row.

Shape armholes
Cast off 5(6, 6, 7, 8, 9) sts at beg next 2 rows, and 3(4, 4, 4, 4, 4) sts at beg foll 2 rows. (82(84, 88, 90, 94, 96) sts)
Dec 1 st at each end of next 3 rows and 4(4, 5, 5, 6, 6) foll alt rows. (68(70, 72, 74, 76, 78) sts)
Cont without further shaping until armhole measures 18(18, 19, 19, 20, 20) cm **(7(7, 7½, 7½, 8, 8)in)**, ending with RS facing for next row.

Shape shoulders and back neck
Cast off 4(5, 5, 5, 6, 6) sts at beg next 2 rows.
Cast off 4(5, 5, 5, 6, 6) sts, patt until there are 8(7, 8, 9, 8, 9) sts on RH needle and turn, leaving rem sts on a holder.
Work both sides of neck separately.

Cast off 3 sts, patt to end.
Cast off rem 5(4, 5, 6, 5, 6) sts.
With RS facing rejoin yarn to sts from holder, cast off center 36 sts, patt to end.
Complete to match first side, reversing shapings.

Left front

Using 4.5 mm (US 7) needles cast on 49(52, 54, 56, 59, 61) sts.
Work 10 rows from chart for left front beg and ending rows as indicated on chart for appropriate size.
Change to 5 mm (US 8) needles and work 12 rows in cable and rib patt rep from chart.
Rep 12 row cable patt throughout and AT THE SAME TIME dec 1 st at beg of next row and 4 foll 8th rows.
(44(47, 49, 51, 54, 56) sts)
Cont without any further shaping until work measures 26.5 cm **(10½)in)** from cast-on edge, ending with RS facing for next row.
Inc 1 st at beg of next row and 4 foll 8th rows.
(49(52, 54, 56, 59, 61) sts)
Cont without further shaping until work measures 53 cm **(21in)** from cast-on edge, ending with RS facing for next row.

Shape armhole
Cast off 5(6, 6, 7, 8, 9) sts at beg next row, and 3(4, 4, 4, 4, 4) sts at beg foll alt row. (41(42, 44, 45, 47, 48) sts)
Work 1 row.
Dec 1 st at armhole edge of next 3 rows and 4(4, 5, 5, 6, 6) foll alt rows. (34(35, 36, 37, 38, 39) sts)
Work without further shaping until front is 15 rows shorter than back to shoulder, ending with **WS** facing for next row.

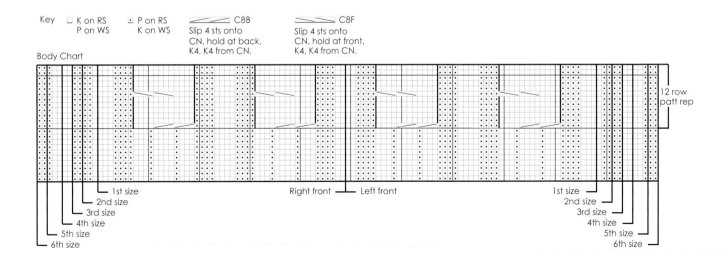

Key   □ K on RS   ⊡ P on RS   C8B   C8F
        P on WS   K on WS   Slip 4 sts onto   Slip 4 sts onto
                                    CN, hold at back,   CN, hold at front,
                                    K4, K4 from CN.   K4, K4 from CN.

Body Chart

12 row patt rep

Right front — Left front

1st size
2nd size
3rd size
4th size
5th size
6th size

Shape front neck

Cast off 10 sts at beg next row and 4 sts at beg foll alt row. (20(21, 22, 23, 24, 25) sts)
Dec 1 st at neck edge on next 4 rows and 3 foll alt rows. (13(14, 15, 16, 17, 18) sts)
Work until front matches back to shoulder, ending with RS facing for next row.

Shape shoulder

Cast off 4(5, 5, 5, 6, 6) sts beg rows and foll alt row.
Work 1 row.
Cast off rem 5(4, 5, 6, 5, 6) sts.

Right front

Using 4.5 mm (US 7) needles cast on 49(52, 54, 56, 59, 61) sts.
Work 10 rows from chart for right front beg and ending rows as indicated on chart for appropriate size.
Change to 5 mm (US 8) needles and work 12 rows in cable and rib patt rep from chart.
Rep 12 row cable patt throughout and AT THE SAME TIME dec 1 st at end of next row and 4 foll 8th rows.
(44(47, 49, 51, 54, 56) sts)
Cont without any further shaping until work measures 26.5 cm (10½)in) from cast-on edge, ending with RS facing for next row.
Inc 1 st at end of next row and 4 foll 8th rows.
(49(52, 54, 56, 59, 61) sts)
Cont without further shaping until work measures 53 cm (21in) from cast-on edge, ending with WS facing for next row.
Complete to match left front, reversing shapings and working an extra row before beg armhole, front neck, and shoulder shaping.

Sleeves (work both the same)

Using 4.5 mm (US 7) needles cast on 50(50, 52, 52, 54, 54) sts.
Rib row 1: K0(0, 0, 0, 1, 1) P3(3, 4, 4, 4, 4), (K4, P4) twice, K3, P1, K4, P1, K3, (P4, K4) twice, P3(3, 4, 4, 4, 4), K0(0, 0, 0, 1, 1).
Rib row 2: P0(0, 0, 0, 1, 1) K3(3, 4, 4, 4, 4), (P4, K4) twice, P3, K1, P4, K1, P3, (K4, P4) twice, K3(3, 4, 4, 4, 4), P0(0, 0, 0, 1, 1).
These 2 rows form rib.
Work in rib for a further 9 rows, ending with WS facing for next row.
Inc 1 st at each end of next row. (52(52, 54, 54, 56, 56) sts)
Change to 5 mm (US 8) needles and work 12 rows in cable and rib patt setting sts as folls:
Row 1: K0(0, 1, 1, 2, 2), P4, (K4, P4) twice, C8B, K4, (P4, K4) twice, P4, K0(0, 1, 1, 2, 2).
Row 2 and every alt row: P0(0, 1, 1, 2, 2), K4, (P4, K4) twice, P12, (K4, P4) twice, K4, P0(0, 1, 1, 2, 2).
Row 3: K0(0, 1, 1, 2, 2), P4, (K4, P4) twice, K12, (P4, K4) twice, P4, K0(0, 1, 1, 2, 2).

Row 5: As row 3.
Row 7: K0(0, 1, 1, 2, 2), P4, (K4, P4) twice, K4, C8F, (P4, K4) twice, P4, K0(0, 1, 1, 2, 2).
Row 9: As row 3.
Row 11: As row 3.
Row 12: P0(0, 1, 1, 2, 2), K4, (P4, K4) twice, P12, (K4, P4) twice, K4, P0(0, 1, 1, 2, 2).
These 12 rows form the patt.
Work 8(8, 4, 4, 2, 2) rows in patt ending with RS facing for next row.
Inc 1 st at each end of next row and every foll 20th (20th, 16th, 16th, 14th, 14th)row to 60(60, 64, 64, 68, 68) sts.
Work without further shaping until work measures 45.5(45.5, 48.5, 48.5, 51, 51) cm **(18(18, 19, 19, 20, 20)in)** from cast on, ending with RS facing for next row.

Shape sleevehead

Cast off 5 sts at beg next 2 rows. (50(50, 54, 54, 58, 58) sts)
Dec 1 st at each end of next 3 rows and 3 foll alt rows. (38(38, 42, 42, 46, 46) sts)
Work 3 rows.
Dec 1 st at each end of next row and 2 foll 4th rows. (32(32, 36, 36, 40, 40) sts)
Work 1 row.
Dec 1 st at each end of next row and foll alt row, then on every foll row to (22(22, 26, 26, 30, 30)) sts.
Cast off 3 sts at beg next 4 rows. (10(10, 14, 14, 18, 18) sts)
Cast off rem sts, dec 3 sts across cable.

Making up

Press/block as described in finishing techniques (pg 158).
Join both shoulder seams using back stitch.

Neckband

With RS of right front facing and using 4.5 mm (US 7) needles pick up and K 22 sts up right front neck to shoulder, 37 sts across back neck and 22 sts down left front neck. (81 sts)
Next row (WS): (P3, K3) to last 3 sts, P3.
Next row: (K3, P3) to last 3 sts, K3.
These 2 rows form rib.
Work 17 rows more in rib.
Cast off in rib.

Right front band

With RS of right front facing and using 4.5 mm (US 7) needles pick up and K 110(110, 112, 112, 114, 114) sts up right front to neck band, and 14 sts from neck band. (124(124, 126, 126, 128, 128) sts)
Work 2 rows in garter st.
Cast off Kwise on **WS**, making button loops as folls:
*Cast off 14 sts, **make button loop:** using last cast-off st make a chain of 4 sts—using the last st cast off—1 st on RH needle, * insert LH needle into this st, knit the stitch—1 st on RH needle, rep from * 3 times more—chain made, 1 st on RH needle.

Pick up last cast-off st with LH needle, knit this st again, take last st of chain over this st, (button loop made). Work from * 7 times, cast off rem sts.

LEFT FRONT BAND
With RS of right front facing and using 4.5 mm (US 7) needles pick up K 14 sts from neck band and K110(110, 112, 112, 114, 114) sts down left front to cast-on edge. (124(124, 126, 126, 128, 128) sts)
Work 2 rows in garter st.
Cast off Kwise on **WS**.
Join side and sleeve seams.
Place center of cast-off edge of sleeve to shoulder seam. Set in sleeve, easing sleevehead into armhole.
Sew on buttons to correspond with button loops.

TWISTED CORD BELT
Twisted cord is made as folls: Cut 8 x 6 meter **(19¾ feet)** lengths of yarn. Knot the strands together at each end. Attach one end to a hook or door handle, insert a knitting needle through the other end. Twist the needle— the tighter the twisting, the firmer the finished cord will be. Hold the cord in the center with one hand (you may need some help); bring both ends of cord together, allowing the two halves to twist together. Keep the cord straight and avoid tangling. Knot the cut ends together and trim. This will make a belt approx 2 meters **(6½ feet)** long.

BELT LOOPS (make 2)
Using 1 strand yarn make a 8 cm **(3 in)** length of chain cording—with a slip knot in right hand, *pull yarn through to make a new slip knot, rep from * until chain is the reqired length. This takes a little practice to get an even tension.
Attach this at side seam, and thread through belt.

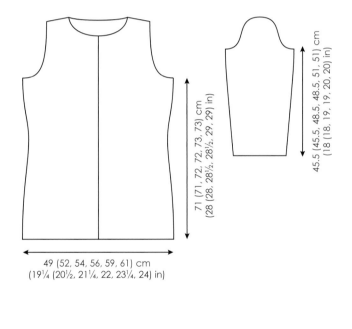

71 (71, 72, 72, 73, 73) cm
(28 (28, 28½, 28½, 29, 29) in)

45.5 (45.5, 48.5, 48.5, 51, 51) cm
(18 (18, 19, 19, 20, 20) in)

49 (52, 54, 56, 59, 61) cm
(19¼ (20½, 21¼, 22, 23¼, 24) in)

KITTY

This allover cable and eyelet pattern looks very complex but is, in fact, deceptively easy. The small cables are mock cables created by knitting stitches together on one row and working a yarn over on the following. Originally photographed in the Summer Classics collection in a cotton-linen blend yarn, the cable lays quite flat, whereas when knitted in a silk-wool blend the cable bounces to life. It is very exciting to see how different yarns react to different stitch patterns.

TO FIT DRESS SIZE:

8	10	12	14	16	18	**US**
10	12	14	16	18	20	**UK**
38	40	42	44	46	48	**EU**

ACTUAL SIZE: Ease allowance approx 10 cm (4 in)

93	98	102	107	111	116	cm
36½	38½	40	42	43¾	45¾	in

FINISHED LENGTH:

56	56	58.5	58.5	61	61	cm
22	22	23	23	24	24	in

SLEEVE LENGTH:

35.5	35.5	38	38	40.5	40.5	cm
14	14	15	15	16	16	in

YARN
Knitted in worsted-weight yarn
2nd size photographed in Louisa Harding Cinnabar sh. 11 White

12	13	13	14	14	15	x 50g balls

1st size photographed in Louisa Harding Grace sh. 8 Teal

9	10	10	11	11	12	x 50g balls

NEEDLES
Pair of 4 mm (US 6) knitting needles
Pair of 5 mm (US 8) knitting needles
Cable needle

BUTTONS
12(12, 12, 12, 13, 13) small mother of pearl

TENSION/GAUGE
22 sts x 24 rows to 10 cm (4 in) square measured over cable patt using 5 mm (US 8) knitting needles

NOTE
Do not work any incomplete cable patterns when shaping armholes and front neck, work these stitches in stocking stitch.

BACK

Using 4 mm (US 6) needles work picot cast on-as folls:
*Cast on 5 sts using the cable cast-on method, cast off
2 sts, slip st on RH needle back onto LH needle
(3 sts now on LH needle), rep from * until there are
102(108, 111, 117, 120, 126) sts on needle, cast on
0(0, 1, 1, 2, 2) sts. (102(108, 112, 118, 122, 128) sts)
Rib row 1: K0(3, 0, 3, 0, 3), (P2, K3) 20(20, 22, 22, 24, 24)
times, P2, K0(3, 0, 3, 0, 3).
Rib row 2: P0(3, 0, 3, 0, 3), (K2, P3) 20(20, 22, 22, 24, 24)
times, K2, P0(3, 0, 3, 0, 3).
Rib row 3 (dec): K0(3, 0, 3, 0, 3), (P2, sl1, K2, psso)
20(20, 22, 22, 24, 24) times, P2, K0(3, 0, 3, 0, 3).
Rib row 4 (inc): P0(3, 0, 3, 0, 3), (K2, P1, yo, P1)
20(20, 22, 22, 24, 24) times, K2, P0(3, 0, 3, 0, 3).
These 4 rows form rib.
Cont in rib as set until chart row 34 is completed.
Change to 5 mm (US 8) needles and cont to work from
chart until chart row 50 is completed.
The last 16 rows form the cable patt rep and are
repeated throughout.
Cont in cable patt until work measures 38(38, 39.5, 39.5,
41, 41) cm **(15(15, 15½, 15½, 16, 16) in)** from cast-on
edge, ending with RS facing for next row.

SHAPE ARMHOLES
Keeping patt correct, cast off 4(6, 6, 6, 6, 8) sts at beg of
next 2 rows and 4 sts at beg of 2 foll rows.
(86(88, 92, 98, 102, 104) sts)
Dec 1 st at each end of next row and 3(3, 3, 5, 5, 5) foll
alt rows. (78(80, 84, 86, 90, 92) sts)

Cont without further shaping until armhole measures
18(18, 19, 19, 20, 20) cm **(7(7, 7½, 7½, 8, 8) in)**, ending
with RS facing for next row.

SHAPE SHOULDERS AND BACK NECK
Cast off 7(8, 8, 9, 9, 10) sts at beg of next 2 rows.
(64(64, 68, 68, 72, 72) sts)

SHAPE RIGHT SHOULDER AND BACK NECK
Next row: Cast off 7(8, 8, 9, 9, 10) sts, patt until there are
11(10, 12, 11, 13, 12) sts on RH needle, turn, leave rem sts
on a holder for left shoulder and back neck.
Next row: Cast off 3 sts, patt to end.
Cast off rem 8(7, 9, 8, 10, 9) sts.
With RS facing, rejoin yarn to rem sts, cast off center
28 sts, patt to end.

SHAPE LEFT SHOULDER AND BACK NECK
Next row: Cast off 7(8, 8, 9, 9, 10) sts, patt to end.
Next row: Cast off 3 sts, patt to end.
Cast off rem 8(7, 9, 8, 10, 9) sts.

LEFT FRONT

Using 4 mm (US 6) needles work picot cast-on as folls:
*Cast on 5 sts using the cable cast-on method, cast off
2 sts, slip st on RH needle back onto LH needle
(3 sts now on LH needle), rep from * until there are 51(54,
54, 57, 60, 63) sts on needle, cast on 0(0, 2, 2, 1, 1) sts.
(51(54, 56, 59, 61, 64) sts)

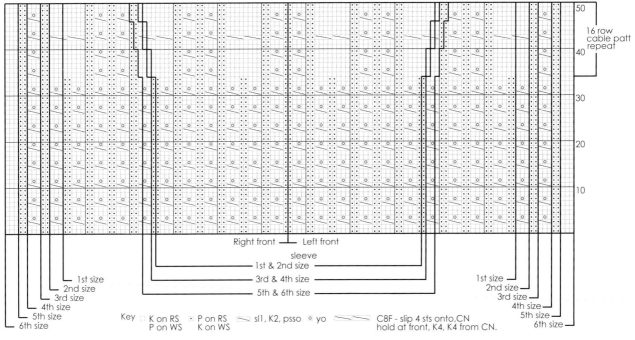

Key: ☐ K on RS / P on WS   • P on RS / K on WS   ⟍ sl1, K2, psso   ○ yo   C8F - slip 4 sts onto CN hold at front, K4, K4 from CN.

Note: Do not work any incomplete cables, work these in stocking stitch

Rib row 1: K0(3, 0, 3, 0, 3), (P2, K3) 10(10, 11, 11, 12, 12) times, P1.
Rib row 2: K1, (P3, K2) 10(10, 11, 11, 12, 12) times, P0(3, 0, 3, 0, 3).
Rib row 3 (dec): K0(3, 0, 3, 0, 3), (P2, sl1, K2, psso) 10(10, 11, 11, 12, 12) times, P1.
Rib row 4 (inc): K1, (P1, yo, P1, K2) 10(10, 11, 11, 12, 12) times, P0(3, 0, 3, 0, 3).
These 4 rows form rib.
Cont in rib as set until chart row 34 is completed.
Change to 5 mm (US 8) needles and cont to work from chart until chart row 50 is completed.
The last 16 rows form the cable patt rep and are repeated throughout.
Cont in cable patt until work measures 38(38, 39.5, 39.5, 41, 41) cm **(15(15, 15½, 15½, 16, 16) in)** from cast-on edge, ending with RS facing for next row.

SHAPE ARMHOLE AND FRONT NECK

Keeping patt correct, cast off 4(6, 6, 6, 6, 8) sts at beg of next row and 4 sts at beg of foll alt row.
(43(44, 46, 49, 51, 52) sts)
Work 1 row.
Dec 1 st at each end of next row and 3(3, 3, 5, 5, 5) foll alt rows. (35(36, 38, 37, 39, 40) sts)
Work 1 row.
Dec 1 st at neck edge on next row and 12(12, 12, 10, 10, 10) foll alt rows. (22(23, 25, 26, 28, 29) sts)
Cont without further shaping until armhole measures 18(18, 19, 19, 20, 20) cm **(7(7, 7½, 7½, 8, 8) in)**, ending with RS facing for next row.

SHAPE SHOULDER

Cast off 7(8, 8, 9, 9, 10) sts at beg of next row and foll alt row.
Work 1 row.
Cast off rem 8(7, 9, 8, 10, 9) sts.

RIGHT FRONT

Using 4 mm (US 6) needles work picot cast-on as folls:
*Cast on 5 sts using the cable cast-on method, cast off 2 sts, slip st on RH needle back onto LH needle (3 sts now on LH needle), rep from * until there are 51(54, 54, 57, 60, 63) sts on needle, cast on 0(0, 2, 2, 1, 1) sts. (51(54, 56, 59, 61, 64) sts)
Rib row 1: P1, (K3, P2) 10(10, 11, 11, 12, 12) times, K0(3, 0, 3, 0, 3).
Rib row 2: P0(3, 0, 3, 0, 3), (K2, P3) 10(10, 11, 11, 12, 12) times, K1.
Rib row 3 (dec): P1, (sl1, K2, psso, P2) 10(10, 11, 11, 12, 12) times, K0(3, 0, 3, 0, 3).
Rib row 4 (inc): P0(3, 0, 3, 0, 3), (K2, P1, yo, P1) 10(10, 11, 11, 12, 12) times, K1.
These 4 rows form rib.
Cont in rib as set until chart row 34 is completed.
Change to 5 mm (US 8) needles and cont to work from

chart until chart row 50 is completed.
The last 16 rows form the cable patt rep and are repeated throughout.
Cont in cable patt until work measures 38(38, 39.5, 39.5, 41, 41) cm **(15(15, 15½, 15½, 16, 16) in)** from cast-on edge, ending with **WS** facing for next row.

Shape armhole and front neck
Keeping patt correct, cast off 4(6, 6, 6, 6, 8) sts at beg of next row and 4 sts at beg of foll alt row.
(43(44, 46, 49, 51, 52) sts)
Dec 1 st at each end of next row and 3(3, 3, 5, 5, 5) foll alt rows. (35(36, 38, 37, 39, 40) sts)
Work 1 row.
Dec 1 st at neck edge on next row and 12(12, 12, 10, 10, 10) foll alt rows. (22(23, 25, 26, 28, 29) sts)
Cont without further shaping until armhole measures 18(18, 19, 19, 20, 20) cm **(7(7, 7½, 7½, 8, 8) in)**, ending with **WS** facing for next row.

Shape shoulder
Cast off 7(8, 8, 9, 9, 10) sts at beg of next row and foll alt row.
Work 1 row.
Cast off rem 8(7, 9, 8, 10, 9) sts.

Sleeves (work both the same)

Using 4 mm (US 6) needles work picot cast-on as folls:
*Cast on 5 sts using the cable cast-on method, cast off 2 sts, slip st on RH needle back onto LH needle (3 sts now on LH needle), rep from * until there are 60(60, 60, 60, 66, 66) sts on needle, cast on 0(0, 2, 2, 0, 0) sts.
(60(60, 62, 62, 66, 66) sts)
Rib row 1: K0(0, 0, 0, 2, 2), P1(1, 2, 2, 2, 2), (K3, P2) 11(11, 12, 12, 12, 12) times, K3(3, 0, 0, 2, 2), P1(1, 0, 0, 0, 0).
Rib row 2: P0(0, 0, 0, 2, 2), K1(1, 2, 2, 2, 2), (P3, K2) 11(11, 12, 12, 12, 12) times, P3(3, 0, 0, 2, 2), K1(1, 0, 0, 0, 0).
Rib row 3 (dec): K0(0, 0, 0, 2, 2), P1(1, 2, 2, 2, 2), (sl1, K2, psso, P2) 11(11, 12, 12, 12, 12) times, (sl1, K2, psso) 1(1, 0, 0, 0, 0) times, K0(0, 0, 0, 2, 2), P1(1, 0, 0, 0, 0).
Rib row 4 (inc): P0(0, 0, 0, 2, 2), K1(1, 2, 2, 2, 2), (P1, yo, P1, K2) 11(11, 12, 12, 12, 12) times, (P1, yo, P1) 1(1, 0, 0, 0, 0) times, P0(0, 0, 0, 2, 2), K1(1, 0, 0, 0, 0).
These 4 rows form rib.
Cont in rib as set until chart row 34 is completed.
Change to 5 mm (US 8) needles and cont to work from chart until chart row 50 is completed, rep the last 16 row cable patt rep **at the same time** inc 1 st at each end of chart row 35, 41, and 47 and every foll 6th row to 72(72, 74, 74, 78, 78) sts.
Cont in cable patt without further shaping until work measures 35.5(35.5, 38, 38, 40.5, 40.5) cm **(14(14, 15, 15, 16, 16) in)** from cast on edge, ending with RS facing for next row.

Shape sleevehead
Keeping patt correct, cast off 5(5, 6, 6, 7, 7) sts at beg of

next 2 rows and 3 sts at beg of 2 foll rows.
(56(56, 56, 56, 58, 58) sts)
Dec 1 st at each end of next 3 rows and 11 foll alt rows, ending with **WS** facing for next row.
(28(28, 28, 28, 30, 30) sts)
Dec 1 st at each end of next row. (26(26, 26, 26, 28, 28) sts)
Cast off 4 sts at beg of next 4 rows.
Cast off rem 10(10, 10, 10, 12, 12) sts.

Making up

Press/block as described in finishing techniques (pg 158).
Join shoulder seams.

Right front band
With RS of right front facing and using 4 mm (US 6) needles, pick up and knit 76(76, 78, 78, 80, 80) sts up right front to start of neck shaping, 40(40, 42, 42, 44, 44) sts to shoulder, 17 sts across to center back neck.
(133(133, 137, 137, 141, 141 sts)
Work 2 rows in garter st.
Cast off Kwise on **WS**, making button loops as folls:
Cast off 57(57, 59, 59, 61, 61) sts, * **make button loop:** using last cast-off st make a chain of 4 sts—using the last st cast off—1 st on RH needle, (insert LH needle into this st, knit the stitch—1 st on RH needle) 4 times more—chain made, 1 st on RH needle. Pick up last cast off st with LH needle, knit this st again, take last st of chain over this st, (button loop made), cast off 6 sts, rep from * 10(10, 10, 10, 11, 11) times more, **make button loop**, cast off rem sts.

Left front band
With RS of back neck facing and using 4 mm (US 6) needles pick up and K 17 sts from center back neck to shoulder, 40(40, 42, 42, 44, 44) sts to start of left front neck shaping and 76(76, 78, 78, 80, 80) sts down left front to cast-on edge. (133(133, 137, 137, 141, 141 sts)
Work 2 rows in garter st.
Cast off Kwise on **WS**.
Join side and sleeve seams.
Place center of cast-off edge of sleeve to shoulder seam. Set in sleeve, easing sleevehead into armhole.
Sew on buttons to correspond with button loops.

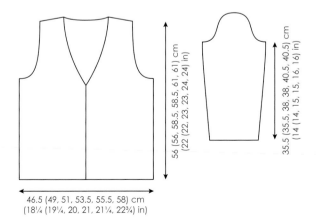

46.5 (49, 51, 53.5, 55.5, 58) cm
(18¼ (19¼, 20, 21, 21¼, 22¾) in)

56 (56, 58.5, 58.5, 61, 61) cm
(22 (22, 23, 23, 24, 24) in)

35.5 (35.5, 38, 38, 40.5, 40.5) cm
(14 (14, 15, 15, 16, 16) in)

ALWAR

This design comes from my Rajasthan collection. I love the elegance of this allover lace cardigan and the unusual addition of clasps as front fastenings. So as not to disrupt the lace pattern, it is worked in one piece up to the armholes and all the edgings are worked at the same time as the main body piece. The lace stitch is enhanced by the choice of a silk yarn, and the drape of the fabric is understated and sophisticated.

To fit dress size:

8–10	12–14	16–18	**US**
10–12	14–16	18–20	**UK**
38–40	42–44	46–48	**EU**

Actual size: Ease allowance approx 6.5–10 cm (2½–4 in)

87.5	102.5	117	cm
34½	40½	46	in

Finished length:

54	54	54	cm
21¼	21¼	21¼	in

Sleeve length:

44	44	44	cm
17¼	17¼	17¼	in

Yarn

Knitted in double knitting–weight yarn
1st size photographed in Louisa Harding Mulberry sh. 16 Teal

9	10	11	x 50g balls

Needles

Pair of 3.25 mm (US 3) circular knitting needles
Pair of 3.25 mm (US 3) knitting needles
Pair of 4 mm (US 6) circular knitting needles
Pair of 4 mm (US 6) knitting needles

Note

Because of the large number of sts on the needles for back & fronts I suggest using pairs of circular needles.

Extras

5 small clasps

Tension/gauge

22 sts x 32 rows to 10cm (4in) square measured over lace pattern using 4 mm (US 6) knitting needles

BACK & FRONTS (knitted in one piece to armholes)

Using 3.25 mm (US 3) circular needles cast on 193(225, 257) sts.
Row 1 (RS): (K1, P1) to last st, K1.
Row 2: (K1, P1) to last st, K1.
These 2 rows form moss st.
Work in moss st until work measures 4 cm **(1½ in)** from cast-on edge, ending with RS facing for next row.
Change to 4 mm (US 6) circular needles and work from chart and written instructions setting sts as follows:
Chart row 1 (RS): (K1, P1) 4 times, K1, yo, K2tog tbl, K2, (K1, K2tog, yo, K1, yo, K2tog tbl, K2) 21(25, 29) times, K1, K2tog, yo, K1, (P1, K1) 4 times.
Chart row 2 and 5 foll WS rows: (K1, P1) 3 times, K1, P to last 7 sts, K1, (P1, K1) 3 times.
Chart row 3: (K1, P1) 4 times, K2, yo, K2tog tbl, K1, (K2tog, yo, K3, yo, K2tog tbl, K1) 21(25, 29) times, K2tog, yo, K2, (P1, K1) 4 times.
Chart row 5: (K1, P1) 4 times, K3, yo, sl1, K2tog, psso, (yo, K5, yo, sl1, K2tog, psso) 21(25, 29) times, yo, K3, (P1, K1) 4 times.
Chart row 7: (K1, P1) 4 times, K2, K2tog, yo, K1, (yo, K2tog tbl, K3, K2tog, yo, K1) 21(25, 29) times, yo, Ktog tbl, K2, (P1, K1) 4 times.
Chart row 9: (K1, P1) 4 times, K1, K2tog, yo, K2, (K1, yo, K2tog tbl, K1, K2tog, yo, K2) 21(25, 29) times, K1, yo, K2tog tbl, K1, (P1, K1) 4 times.
Chart row 11: (K1, P1) 4 times, K2tog, yo, K3, (K2, yo, sl1, K2tog, psso, yo, K3) 21(25, 29) times, K2, yo, K2tog tbl, (P1, K1) 4 times.
Chart row 13: (K1, P1) to last st, K1.
Chart row 14: (K1, P1) to last st, K1.
Chart row 15: (K1, P1) to last st, K1.
Chart row 16: (K1, P1) to last st, K1.
These 16 rows form the lace and moss st pattern with moss st edge.
Rep the 16 row patt rep 5 times more, ending with row 16 and RS facing for next row.

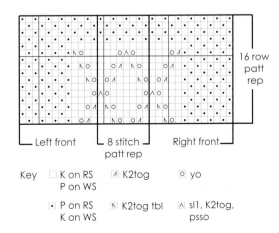

Left front — 8 stitch patt rep — Right front

Key
☐ K on RS P on WS
⊡ P on RS K on WS
☑ K2tog
☒ K2tog tbl
⊙ yo
⋀ sl1, K2tog, psso

DIVIDE FOR RIGHT FRONT

Next row (chart row 1) (RS): Patt 34(42, 50) sts, turn, leave rem sts on a holder for back and left front.
Next row (chart row 2) (WS): K1, patt 33(41, 49) sts as sts set.
Next row (chart row 3) (RS): Patt 33(41, 49) sts as sts set, K1.
Next row (chart row 4): K1, patt 33(41, 49) sts as sts set.
These last 2 rows set the pattern with armhole edge in knit selvedge st.
Cont until chart row 16 is completed.
Rep 16 row patt rep twice more.

SHAPE RIGHT FRONT NECK AND SHOULDER

Next row (chart row 1) (RS): Cast off 16 sts, (1 st on RH needle) (P1, K1) 3 times, P1, patt 9(17, 25), K1. (18(26, 34) sts)
Next row (chart row 2): K1, patt 9(17, 25), (P1, K1) 4 times.
These last 2 rows set the pattern with neck edge worked in moss st and armhole edge in knit selvedge st.
Cont until chart row 16 is completed, ending with RS facing for next row.
Leave sts on a holder.

BACK

With RS facing, rejoin yarn to rem sts on holder for back and left front, cast off 29 sts, patt until there are 67(83, 99) sts on RH needle, turn, leave rem sts on a holder for left front.
Next row (chart row 2) (WS): K1, patt 65(81, 97) sts in patt as sts set, K1.
Next row (chart row 3) (RS): K1, patt 65(81, 97) sts, in patt as set, K1.
Next row (chart row 4): K1, patt 65(81, 97) sts in patt as sts set, K1.
These last 2 rows set the pattern with armhole edges in knit selvedge st.
Cont until chart row 16 is completed.
Rep 16 row patt rep twice more.

SHAPE RIGHT BACK NECK AND SHOULDER

Next row (chart row 1) (RS): K1, patt 9(17, 25), (P1, K1) 4 times, turn, leave rem sts on a holder for back neck and right shoulder. (18(26, 34) sts)
Next row (chart row 2): (K1, P1) 4 times, patt 9(17, 25), K1.
These last 2 rows set the pattern with neck edge worked in moss st and armhole edge in knit selvedge st.
Cont until chart row 16 is completed, ending with RS facing for next row.
Leave sts on a holder.
With RS facing, rejoin yarn to rem sts on holder for back neck and left back neck and shoulder, cast off 31 sts, (1 st on RH needle), (P1, K1) 3 times, P1, patt 9(17, 25), K1. (18(26, 34) sts)
Next row (chart row 2) (WS): K1, patt 9(17, 25), (P1, K1) 4 times.
Next row (chart row 3) (RS): (K1, P1) 4 times, patt 9(17, 25) sts, K1.
Next row (chart row 4): K1, patt 9(17, 25), (P1, K1) 4 times.

These last 2 rows set the pattern with armhole edges in knit selvedge st.
Cont until chart row 16 completed, ending with RS facing for next row.
Leave sts on a holder.

LEFT FRONT

With RS facing, rejoin yarn to rem sts on holder for left front, cast off 29 sts (1 st on RH needle), patt to end (34(42, 50) sts).
Next row (chart row 2) (WS): Patt 33(41, 49) sts as sts set, K1.
Next row (chart row 3) (RS): K1, patt 33(41, 49) sts as sts set.
Next row (chart row 4): Patt 33(41, 49) sts as sts set, K1.
These last 2 rows set the pattern with armhole edge in knit selvedge st.
Cont until chart row 16 is completed.
Rep 16 row patt rep twice more.

SHAPE LEFT FRONT NECK AND SHOULDER

Next row (chart row 1) (RS): K1, patt 9(17, 25), (P1, K1) 12 times.
Next row (chart row 2) (WS): Cast off 16 sts, (1 st on RH needle) (P1, K1) 3 times, P1, patt 9(17, 25), K1. (18(26, 34) sts)
Next row (chart row 3): K1, patt 9(17, 25), (P1, K1) 4 times.
Next row (chart row 4): (K1, P1) 4 times, patt 9(17, 25), K1.
These last 2 rows set the pattern with neck edge worked in moss st and armhole edge in knit selvedge st.
Cont until chart row 16 is completed, ending with RS facing for next row.
Leave sts on a holder.

SLEEVES (work both the same)

Using 3.25 mm (US 3) needles cast on 91 sts.
Row 1 (RS): (K1, P1) to last st, K1.
Row 2: (K1, P1) to last st, K1.
These 2 rows form moss st.
Work in moss st until work measures 4 cm **(1½ in)** from cast-on edge, ending with RS facing for next row.

Change to 4 mm (US 6) needles and work from chart and written instructions setting sts as follows:
Chart row 1 (RS): K2, yo, K2tog tbl, K2, (K1, K2tog, yo, K1, yo, K2tog tbl, K2) 10 times, K1, K2tog, yo, K2.
Chart row 2 and 5 foll WS rows: K1, P to last st, K1.
Chart row 3: K3, yo, K2tog tbl, K1, (K2tog, yo, K3, yo, K2tog tbl, K1) 10 times, K2tog, yo, K3.
Chart row 5: K4, yo, sl1, K2tog, psso, (yo, K5, yo, sl1, K2tog, psso) 10 times, yo, K4.
Chart row 7: K3, K2tog, yo, K1, (yo, K2tog tbl, K3, K2tog, yo, K1) 10 times, yo, Ktog tbl, K3.
Chart row 9: K2, K2tog, yo, K2, (K1, yo, K2tog tbl, K1, K2tog, yo, K2) 10 times, K1, yo, K2tog tbl, K2.
Chart row 11: K1, K2tog, yo, K3, (K2, yo, sl1, K2tog, psso, yo, K3) 10 times, K2, yo, K2tog tbl, K1.
Chart row 13: (P1, K1) to last st, P1.
Chart row 14: (P1, K1) to last st, P1.
Chart row 15: (P1, K1) to last st, P1.
Chart row 16: (P1, K1) to last st, P1.
These 16 rows form the lace and moss st pattern.
Rep the 16 row patt rep 7 times more, ending with row 16 and RS facing for next row.
Cast off in moss st.

MAKING UP

Press/block as described in finishing techniques (pg 158).
With RS together join right shoulder seam using 3 needle cast-off.
Join left shoulder seam as above.
Place a marker on sleeves edges 7.5 cm **(3 in)** down from cast-on edge.
Join sleeve seams up to marker.
Set sleeves into armholes using the square set-in method.
Place center of cast-off edge of sleeve to shoulder seam. Sew cast-off edge of sleeve to armhole edge of garment.
Making a neat right angle, sew straight sides at top of sleeve to cast-off sts at armhole.
Using photograph as a guide sew clasps into position on fronts.

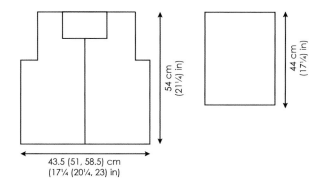

43.5 (51, 58.5) cm
(17¼ (20¼, 23) in)

54 cm (21¼ in)

44 cm (17¼ in)

Dressing Up

The aim of this chapter is to dispel the myth that the cardigan is nothing more than a core work-a-day staple of the wardrobe. When knitted in exciting yarns, embellished creatively, and worn with a bit of flair and creativity, the cardigan is the ideal garment to dress up. The patterns here were created with the exclusive purpose of spicing up the sweater—and the girl in it!

I've often said that as we women grow older we never lose sight of our inner "Barbie." We just suppress it. I am hereby dusting off that tiara. Now go experiment with interesting yarn combinations, explore adding embroidery to your knitting, embellish with something pretty, and, finally, release the creative inner you.

CECILE

Originally I used a variegated ribbon yarn as the main yarn in this design. I picked out a Sari Ribbon shade
that complemented the variation and made for this unusual design combination. When I remade it, I wanted the
cables to become the prominent feature, so I used Kashmir Aran, ideal for showing off stitch structure.
Once again, you'll see the Sari Ribbon for the edging detail.

TO FIT DRESS SIZE:

8–10	12	14	16–18	**US**
10–12	14	16	18–20	**UK**
38–40	42	44	46–48	**EU**

ACTUAL SIZE: Ease allowance approx 5–10 cm (2–4 in)

91	98	102	109	cm
35 ¾	38 ½	40	43	in

FINISHED LENGTH:

45	45	47	47	cm
17 ¾	17 ¾	18 ½	18 ¼	in

SLEEVE LENGTH:

36	36	36	36	cm
14 ¼	14 ¼	14 ¼	14 ¼	in

YARN
Knitted in aran–weight yarn
1st size photographed in Kimono Ribbon and Sari Ribbon
A. Kimono Ribbon sh. 5 Forties

7	7	8	8	x 50g balls

B. Sari Ribbon sh. 1 Red Mix

1	1	1	1	x 50g balls

1st size photographed in Kashmir Aran and Sari Ribbon
A. Kashmir Aran sh. 23 Sage

9	9	10	10	x 50g balls

B. Sari Ribbon sh. 28 Icicle

1	1	1	1	x 50g balls

NEEDLES
Pair of 6 mm (US 10) knitting needles
Pair of 6.5 mm (US 10½) knitting needles
Cable needle
Kashmir Aran garment only
Pair of 5 mm (US 8) knitting needles
Pair of 6.5 mm (US 10½) knitting needles
Cable needle

TENSION/GAUGE
Kimono Ribbon garment
18 sts x 24 rows to 10 cm (4 in) square measured over
st st using 6 mm (US 10) knitting needles.
Kashmir Aran garment
18 sts x 24 rows to 10 cm (4 in) square measured over
st st using 5 mm (US 8) knitting needles.

BACK

Using 6.5 mm (US 10 ½) needles and yarn B work picot cast-on as folls:
Cast on 5 sts, cast off 2 sts, slip st on RH needle back onto LH needle (3 sts now on LH needle) rep from * to * until there are 72(78, 81, 87) sts on needle.
Work 2 rows in garter st, inc 0(0, 1, 1) sts at end of last row. (72(78, 82, 88) sts)
Change to yarn A and smaller size needles and beg with a K row cont in st st as folls:
Work 10 rows, ending with RS facing for next row.
Next row (RS) (inc): K3, M1, K to last 3 sts, M1, K3.
Working all incs as set by last row, cont in st st, inc 1 st at each end of every foll 10th row until there are 82(88, 92, 98) sts.
Cont to work without further shaping until work measures 27(27, 28, 28) cm **10½(10½, 11, 11) in,** ending with RS facing for next row.

SHAPE ARMHOLES

Cast off 4(5, 6, 6) sts at beg next 2 rows, and 3(3, 4, 4) sts at beg foll 2 rows. (68(72, 72, 78) sts)
Dec 1 st at each end of next and every foll alt row until 62(64, 66, 68) sts rem.
Cont without further shaping until armhole measures 18(18, 19, 19) cm **7(7, 7½, 7½) in,** ending with RS facing for next row.

SHAPE SHOULDERS AND BACK NECK

Cast off 6(6, 7, 7) sts at beg next 2 rows.
Cast off 6(6, 7, 7) sts, K until there are 9(10, 9, 10) on RH needle and turn, leaving rem sts on a holder.
Work both sides of neck separately.
Cast off 3 sts, P to end.
Cast off rem 6(7, 6, 7) sts.
With RS facing rejoin yarn to sts from holder, cast off center 20 sts, K to end.
Complete to match first side, reversing shapings and working an extra row before beg of shoulder shaping.

LEFT FRONT

Using 6.5 mm (US 10 ½) needles and yarn B work picot cast-on as folls:
Cast on 5 sts, cast off 2 sts, slip st on RH needle back onto LH needle (3 sts now on LH needle) rep from * to * until there are 36(39, 42, 45) sts on needle.
Work 2 rows in garter st, dec 0(0, 1, 1) sts at end of last row. (36(39, 41, 44) sts)
Change to yarn A and smaller size needles and cont in patt as folls:
Row 1 (RS) (inc): K6(9, 11, 14), P1, K2, P1, K2, M1, K4, M1, K2, P1, K2, P1, K to end. (38(41, 43, 46) sts)
Row 2: P14, K1, P2, K1, P10, K1, P2, K1, P to end.
Row 3: K6(9, 11, 14), P2tog, (yo) twice, P2tog, K10, P2tog, (yo) twice, P2tog, K to end.

Row 4 and every foll alt row: P14, K2, P1, K1, P10, K2, P1, K1, P to end.
Row 5: K6(9, 11, 14) P2tog, (yo) twice, P2tog, C10F, P2tog, (yo) twice, P2tog, K to end.
Rows 7 and 9: As row 3.
Row 11 (RS) (inc): K3, M1, K3(6, 8, 11), P2tog, (yo) twice, P2tog, K10, P2tog, (yo) twice, P2tog, K to end.
Row 13: K7(10, 12, 15), P2tog, (yo) twice, P2tog, K10, P2tog, (yo) twice, P2tog, K14.
Row 14: As row 4.
Rows 3–14 form cable and ladder patt and start side seam shaping.
Cont in patt, inc 1 st at beg of 7th and every foll 10th row until there are 43(46, 48, 51) sts.
Cont to work without further shaping until left front matches back to beg of armhole shaping, ending with RS facing for next row.

SHAPE ARMHOLE

Cast off 4(5, 6, 6) sts at beg next row, and 3(3, 4, 4) sts at beg foll alt row. 36(38, 38, 41) sts)
Work 1 row.
Dec 1 st at beg of next and every foll alt row until 33(34, 35, 36) sts rem.
Cont without further shaping until 13 rows less have been worked than on back to start of shoulder shaping, ending with **WS** facing for next row.

SHAPE NECK

Cast off 5 sts at beg next row and 3 sts at beg foll alt row.
Dec 1 st at neck edge next 3 rows and 2 foll alt rows. 20(21, 22, 23) sts.
Cont straight until left front matches back to start of shoulder shaping, ending with RS facing for next row.

SHAPE SHOULDER

Working (K2tog) twice across top of cables, cast off 6(6, 7, 7) sts at beg next row and foll alt row.
Work 1 row.
Cast off rem 6(7, 6, 7) sts.

RIGHT FRONT

Using 6.5 mm (US 10 ½) needles and yarn B work picot cast-on as folls:
Cast on 5 sts, cast off 2 sts, slip st on RH needle back onto LH needle (3 sts now on LH needle) rep from * to * until there are 36(39, 42, 45) sts on needle.
Work 2 rows in garter st, dec 0(0, 1, 1) sts at end of last row.
(36(39, 41, 44) sts)
Change to yarn A and cont in patt as folls:
Row 1 (RS) (inc): K14, P1, K2, P1, K2, M1, K4, M1, K2, P1, K2, P1, K to end.
Row 2: P6(9, 11, 14), K1, P2, K1, P10, K1, P2, K1, P to end.
Row 3: K14, P2tog, (yo) twice, P2tog, K10, P2tog, (yo) twice, P2tog, K to end.

Rows 4, 6, 8, and 10: P6(9, 11, 14), K2, P1, K1, P10, K2, P1, K1, P to end.

Row 5: K14, P2tog, (yo) twice, P2tog, C10B, P2tog, (yo) twice, P2tog, K to end.

Rows 7 and 9: K14, P2tog, (yo) twice, P2tog, K10, P2tog, (yo) twice, P2tog, K to end.

Row 11 (RS) (inc): K14, P2tog, (yo) twice, P2tog, K10, P2tog, (yo) twice, P2tog, to last 3 sts, M1, K3.

Row 12: P7(10, 12, 13), K2, P1, K1, P10, K2, P1, K1, P14.

Row 13: As row 3.

Row 14: As row 12.

Rows 3–14 form cable and ladder patt and start side seam shaping.

Cont in patt, complete to match left front, reversing shapings and working an extra row before beg armhole, neck and shoulder shaping.

SLEEVES (work both the same)

Using 6.5 mm (US 10 ½) needles and yarn B work picot cast-on as folls:

Cast on 5 sts, cast off 2 sts, slip st on RH needle back onto LH needle (3 sts now on LH needle) rep from * to * until there are 45(45, 48, 48) sts on needle.

Work 2 rows in garter st, inc 1(1, 0, 0) sts at end of last row. (46(46, 48, 48) sts)

Change to yarn A and smaller size needles and beg with a K row cont in st st as folls:

Work 12 rows, ending with RS facing for next row.

Next row (RS) (inc): K3, M1, K to last 3 sts, M1, K3.

Working all incs as set by last row, cont in st st, inc 1 st at each end of every foll 10th row until there are 58(58, 62, 62) sts.

Work without further shaping until sleeve measures 36 cm **(14¼ in)**, ending with RS facing for next row.

SHAPE SLEEVEHEAD

Cast off 4 sts at beg next 2 rows, and 3 sts at beg foll 2 rows. (44(44, 48, 48) sts)

Dec 1 st at each end of next 3 rows and foll alt row. (36(36, 40, 40) sts)

Work 3 rows.

Dec 1 st at each end of next row and 3 foll 4th rows. (28(28, 32, 32) sts)

Work 1 row.

Dec 1 st at each end of next row and foll alt row, then on foll row. (22(22, 26, 26) sts)

Cast off 3 sts at beg next 4 rows. (10(10, 14, 14) sts)

Cast off rem sts.

MAKING UP

Press/block as described in finishing techniques (pg 158). Join both shoulder seams using back stitch.

RIGHT FRONT BAND

With RS facing, starting at cast-on edge of right front and using 6.5 mm (US 10½) needles and yarn B, pick up and knit 75(75, 77, 77, 82, 82) sts to start of front neck shaping.

Work 2 rows in garter st.

Cast off Kwise on **WS**.

LEFT FRONT BAND

With RS facing and using 6.5 mm (US 10½) needles, pick up and knit 75(75, 77, 77, 82, 82) sts along left front from start of neck shaping to cast-on edge.

Work 2 rows in garter st.

Cast off Kwise on **WS**.

NECK EDGING

With RS facing and using 6.5 mm (US 10½) needles and yarn B, pick up and knit 20 sts to shoulder, 26 sts across back neck, and 20 sts down left front neck. (66 sts)

Work 2 rows in garter st.

Cast off Kwise on **WS**.

Join side and sleeve seams.

Place center of cast-off edge of sleeve to shoulder seam. Set in sleeve, easing sleevehead into armhole.

TIES

Cut two lengths of yarn B and attach at neck edge or opposite armhole shaping as in photographs.

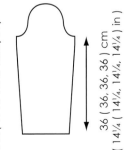

45 (45, 47, 47) cm
(17¾ (17¾, 18½, 18½) in)

36 (36, 36, 36) cm
(14¼ (14¼, 14¼, 14¼) in)

45.5 (49, 51, 54.5) cm
(18 (19¼, 20, 21½) in)

ORCHIS

This very simple bolero is knitted using my Sari Ribbon yarn. It is very quick to knit, as the yarn is bulky weight. When I first saw the Sari Ribbon yarn, I was drawn to it like a magpie. The vibrant ribbon with the metallic core just reminded me of Indian Saris that I had seen when visiting Rajasthan in India. I knew that I wanted to include this yarn in my collection—it appealed to my inner girlyness, as I knew it would appeal to all women.

TO FIT DRESS SIZE:

8	10	12	14	16	18	**US**
10	12	14	16	18	20	**UK**
38	40	42	44	46	48	**EU**

ACTUAL SIZE: Ease allowance approx 5 cm (2 in)

87	90	97	103	107	110	cm
34 ¼	35 ½	38 ¼	40 ½	42	43 ¼	in

FINISHED LENGTH:

43	43	44	44	45	45	cm
17	17	17¼	17¼	17¾	17¾	in

SLEEVE LENGTH:

30	30	32	32	34	34	cm
12	12	12½	12½	13½	13½	in

YARN
Knitted in bulky-weight yarn
1st size photographed in Louisa Harding Sari Ribbon
sh. 6 Silver Olive

7	7	8	8	9	9	x 50g balls

NEEDLES
Pair of 7 mm (US 10½) knitting needles
Pair of 8 mm (US 11) knitting needles
Pair of 7 mm (US 10½) circular needles

TENSION/GAUGE
12 sts x 16 rows to 10 cm (4 in) square measured over st st using 8 mm (US 11) knitting needles.

BACK

Using 8 mm (US 11) needles cast on 46(48, 52, 56, 58, 60) sts.
Beg with a K row cont in st st as folls:
Work 10 rows, ending with RS facing for next row.
Next row (RS) (inc): K3, M1, K to last 3 sts, M1, K3.
Working all incs as set by last row, cont in st st, inc 1 st at each end of every foll 10th row until there are 52(54, 58, 62, 64, 66) sts.
Cont to work without further shaping until work measures 25 cm **10 in,** ending with RS facing for next row.

SHAPE ARMHOLES

Cast off 3(3, 4, 4, 4, 4) sts at beg next 2 rows.
(46(48, 50, 54, 56, 58) sts)
Next row (RS) (dec): K3, K2tog, K to last 5 sts, K2tog tbl, K3.
Working all decs as set by last row, cont in st st, dec 1 st at each end of every foll alt row until 38(40, 42, 44, 46, 48) sts rem.
Cont without further shaping until armhole measures 18(18, 19, 19, 20, 20) cm **7(7, 7½, 7½, 8, 8) in**, ending with RS facing for next row.

SHAPE SHOULDERS AND BACK NECK

Cast off 3(4, 4, 4, 5, 5) sts at beg next 2 rows.
Cast off 3(4, 4, 4, 5, 5) sts, K until there are 7(6, 7, 8, 7, 8) sts on RH needle and turn, leaving rem sts on a holder.
Work both sides of neck separately.
Cast off 3 sts, P to end.
Cast off rem 4(3, 4, 5, 4, 5) sts.
With RS facing rejoin yarn to sts from holder, cast off center 12 sts, K to end.
Complete to match first side, reversing shapings and working an extra row before beg of shoulder shaping.

LEFT FRONT

Using 8 mm (US 11) needles cast on 18(19, 21, 23, 24, 25) sts.
Beg with a K row cont in st st as folls:
Work 2 rows, ending with RS facing for next row.
Next row (RS) (inc): K to last 3 sts, M1, K3.
Working front shaping incs as set by last row, and side seam shapings 3 sts in from edge of work as given for back, cont in st st, inc 1 st at end of 2nd and foll alt row, then on 2 foll 4th rows, and AT THE SAME TIME inc 1 st at beg (side seam edge) of 8th row.
(24(25, 27, 29, 30, 31) sts)
Work 5 rows, ending with RS facing for next row.
Inc 1 st at beg of next and foll 10th row.
(26(27, 29, 31, 32, 33) sts)
Cont to work without further shaping until left front matches back to beg of armhole shaping, ending with RS facing for next row.

SHAPE ARMHOLE AND FRONT NECK

Next row (RS) (dec): Cast off 3(3, 4, 4, 4, 4) sts, K to last 5 sts, K2tog tbl, K3. (22(23, 24, 26, 27, 28) sts)

Work 1 row.
Next row (RS) (dec): K3, K2tog, K to last 5 sts, K2tog tbl, K3.
Working all decs as set by last row, cont in st st, dec 1 st at end (neck edge) of 2nd and 3 foll alt rows, then on 3 foll 4th rows, and AT THE SAME TIME dec 1 st at beg (armhole edge) of 2(2, 2, 3, 3, 3) foll alt rows. (10(11, 12, 13, 14, 15) sts)
Cont without further shaping until left front matches back to start of shoulder shaping, ending with RS facing for next row.

SHAPE SHOULDER

Cast off 3(4, 4, 4, 5, 5) sts at beg next row and foll alt row.
Work 1 row.
Cast off rem 4(3, 4, 5, 4, 5) sts.

RIGHT FRONT

Using 8 mm (US 11) needles cast on 18(19, 21, 23, 24, 25) sts.
Beg with a K row cont in st st as folls:
Work 2 rows, ending with RS facing for next row.
Next row (RS) (inc): K3, 1, K to end.
Working front shaping incs as set by last row, and side seam shapings 3 sts in from edge of work as given for back, complete to match left front, reversing shapings and working an extra row before beg armhole, neck and shoulder shaping.

SLEEVES (work both the same)

Using 7 mm (US 10½) needles cast on 30(30, 32, 32, 34, 34) sts and knit 2 rows, ending with RS facing for next row.
Change to 8mm (US 11) needles and, beg with a K row, cont in st st as folls:
Work 10 rows, ending with RS facing for next row.
Next row (RS) (inc): K3, M1, K to last 3 sts, M1, K3.
Working all incs as set by last row, cont in st st, inc 1 st at each end of every foll 10th row until there are 38(38, 40, 40, 42, 42) sts.
Cont to work without further shaping until sleeve measures 30(30, 32, 32, 34, 34) cm **12(12, 12½, 12½, 13½, 13½) in**, ending with RS facing for next row.

SHAPE SLEEVEHEAD

Cast off 3 sts at beg next 2 rows. (32(32, 34, 34, 36, 36) sts)
Dec 1 st at each end of next row and 2 foll alt rows. (26(26, 28, 28, 30, 30) sts)
Work 3 rows.
Dec1 st at each end of next row and 2 foll 4th rows. (20(20, 22, 22, 24, 24) sts)
Work 1 row.
Dec 1 st at each end of next row and foll alt row, then on foll 3 rows. (10(10, 12, 12, 14, 14) sts.
Cast off rem sts.

MAKING UP

Press/block as described in finishing techniques (pg 158).
Join both shoulder seams and left side seam using
back stitch.

BOLERO EDGINGS

With RS facing, starting at right side seam and using
7 mm (US 10½) circular needle, pick up and K 18(19,
21, 23, 24, 25) sts along right front cast-on edge, 13
sts around curve, 18 sts up right front to start of neck
shaping, 23(23, 24, 24, 25, 25) sts up right front neck to
shoulder, 18 sts from back, 23(23, 24, 24, 25, 25) sts down
left front neck, 18 sts down left front, 13 sts around curve,
18(19, 21, 23, 24, 25) sts along left front cast-on edge,
then 46(48, 52, 56, 58, 60) sts across back.
(208(212, 222, 230, 236, 240) sts)
Knit 1 row, ending with RS facing for next row.
Row 2 (RS) (inc): K20(21, 23, 25, 26, 27), M1, (K4, M1)twice,
K106(106, 108, 108, 110, 110), (M1, K4) twice, M1, K to
end. (214(218, 228, 236, 242, 246) sts)
Cast off Kwise on WS.
Join right side and sleeve seams.
Place center of cast-off edge of sleeve to shoulder
seam. Set in sleeve, easing sleevehead into armhole.

MAKE TIES (both the same)

Cut 150 cm length of yarn.
Fold in half and secure into place on bolero at start of
front neck shaping.
Trim ends of ribbon to prevent fraying.

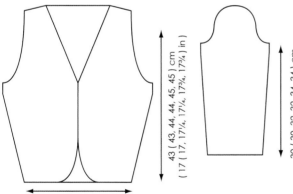

43.5 (45, 48.5, 51.5, 53.5, 55) cm
(17 (17¾, 19, 20¼, 21, 21½) in)

43 (43, 44, 44, 45, 45) cm
(17 (17, 17¼, 17¼, 17¾, 17¾) in)

30 (30, 32, 32, 34, 34) cm
(12 (12, 12½, 12½, 13½, 13½) in)

LACEWING

This design is taken from my Swallowtails collection. The garment is very simple in construction and knitted in squares. The lace edging at the front is inspired by the lightness of a butterfly's wing. Originally photographed in Glisten yarn as the sun came up over the beach in the Algarve in Portugal, this garment really shimmers with the sunrise. I wanted to re-photograph the design in a more contemporary setting and using a cotton-based yarn (my Nautical Cotton), which gives the lace stitch definition and clarity.

TO FIT DRESS SIZE:

8	10	12	14	16	18	**US**
10	12	14	16	18	20	**UK**
38	40	42	44	46	48	**EU**

ACTUAL SIZE: Ease allowance approx 15 cm (6 in)

98	102	106	112	116	120	cm
38½	40¼	41¾	44	45¾	47¼	in

FINISHED LENGTH:

51	51	53.5	53.5	56	56	cm
20	20	21	21	22	22	in

SLEEVE LENGTH:

30.5	30.5	33	33	35.5	35.5	cm
12	12	13	13	14	14	in

YARN

Knitted in worsted-weight yarn
2nd size photographed in Louisa Harding Glisten sh. 23 Rice

12	12	13	14	15	15	x 50g balls

1st size photographed in Louisa Harding Nautical Cotton sh. 14 Marine

12	12	13	14	15	15	x 50g balls

NEEDLES

Glisten yarn
Pair of 4.5 mm (US 7) knitting needles
Pair of 5 mm (US 8) knitting needles
Nautical Cotton yarn
Pair of 4 mm (US 6) knitting needles
Pair of 4.5 mm (US 7) knitting needles

BUTTON

1 medium mother of pearl

TENSION/GAUGE

Glisten yarn
20 sts x 28 rows to 10cm (4 in) square measured over st st using 5 mm (US 8) knitting needles
Nautical Cotton yarn
20 sts x 28 rows to 10cm (4 in) square measured over st st using 4.5 mm (US 8) knitting needles

BACK

Using smallest size needles cast on 98(102, 106, 112, 116, 120) sts.
Starting with a K row work 8 rows in garter st.
Change to 5 mm (US 8) needles and beg with a K row work in st st only until work measures 48.5(48.5, 51, 51, 53.5, 53.5)cm **(19(19, 20, 20, 21, 21)in)** from cast-on edge, ending with RS facing for next row.
Change to 4.5 mm (US 7) needles and work 8 rows in garter st.
Leave sts on a holder.

LEFT FRONT

Using 4.5 mm (US 7) needles cast on 58(60, 62, 65, 67, 69) sts.
Starting with a K row work 8 rows in garter st.
Change to 5 mm (US 8) needles and beg with a K row work in 4 row patt rep setting sts as folls:
Row 1 (RS): Knit.
Row 2: K5, P13, K2, P38(40, 42, 45, 47, 49).
Row 3: K40(42, 44, 47, 49, 51), K4tog, (yo, K1) 5 times, yo, sl 3 sts, k1, pass 3 slip sts over, K5.
Row 4: K5, P13, K2, P38(40, 42, 45, 47, 49).
These 4 rows form the patt.
Cont to work in patt until work measures 48.5(48.5, 51, 51, 53.5, 53.5)cm **(19(19, 20, 20, 21, 21)in)** from cast-on edge, ending with RS facing for next row.
Change to 4.5 mm (US 7) needles and work 4 rows in garter st.
Next row (RS) (buttonhole): K to last 4 sts, yo, K2tog, K2.
Work 2 more rows in garter st.
Next row (WS): Cast off 35 sts, K to end.
Leave rem 23(25, 27, 30, 32, 34) sts on a holder.

RIGHT FRONT

Using 4.5 mm (US 7) needles cast on 58(60, 62, 65, 67, 69) sts.
Starting with a K row work 8 rows in garter st.
Change to 5 mm (US 8) needles and beg with a K row work in 4 row patt rep setting sts as folls:
Row 1 (RS): Knit.
Row 2: P38(40, 42, 45, 47, 49), K2, P13, K5.
Row 3: K5, K4tog, (yo, K1) 5 times, yo, sl 3 sts, k1, pass 3 slip sts over, K40(42, 44, 47, 49, 51).
Row 4: P38(40, 42, 45, 47, 49), K2, P13, K5.
These 4 rows form the patt.
Cont to work in patt until work measures 48.5(48.5, 51, 51, 53.5, 53.5)cm **(19(19, 20, 20, 21, 21)in)** from cast on edge, ending with RS facing for next row.
Change to 4.5 mm (US 7) needles and work 7 rows in garter st.
Next row (WS): K23(25, 27, 30, 32, 34), cast off to end.
Leave rem sts on a holder.

SLEEVES (work both the same)

Using 4.5 mm (US 7) needles cast on 80(80, 84, 84, 88, 88) sts.
Starting with a K row work 4 rows in garter st.
Change to 5 mm (US 8) needles and beg with a K row work in st st only until work measures 23.5(23.5, 26, 26, 28.5, 28.5)cm **(9¼(9¼, 10¼, 10¼, 11¼, 11¼)in)** from cast-on edge, ending with RS facing for next row.
Cast off.

SLEEVE EDGING (work 2)

Using 5 mm (US 8) needles cast on 19 sts and work in 4 row patt rep setting sts as folls:
Row 1 (RS): Knit.
Row 2: K3, P13, K3.
Row 3: K3, K4tog, (yo, K1) 5 times, yo, sl 3 sts, k1, pass 3 slip sts over, K3.
Row 4: K3, P13, K3.
These 4 rows form the patt.
Rep these 4 rows until edging fits around base of sleeve hem.
Cast off.
Stitch into place using mattress stitch or back stitch if preferred.

MAKING UP

Press/block as described in finishing techniques (pg 158).

JOIN SHOULDER SEAMS
With wrong sides of right front and back together, join right shoulder seam by casting off together 23(25, 27, 30, 32, 34) sts from holders, cast off 52 sts from back, cast off together rem 23(25, 27, 30, 32, 34) sts from holders for left shoulder.
Place markers along side edges of Front and Back 20 cm **(8 in)** either side of shoulder seams.
Place center of cast-off edge of sleeves to shoulder seams, then sew sleeves to back and front between markers.
Join side and sleeve seams.
Sew on button at neck edge to correspond with buttonhole. Alternatively I have fastened the garment at the neck with a brooch.

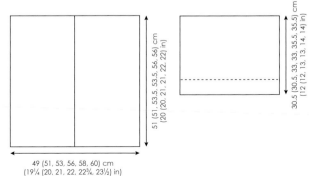

51 (51, 53.5, 53.5, 56, 56) cm
(20 (20, 21, 21, 22, 22) in)

30.5 (30.5, 33, 33, 35.5, 35.5) cm
(12 (12, 13, 13, 14, 14) in)

49 (51, 53, 56, 58, 60) cm
(19¼ (20, 21, 22, 22¾, 23½) in)

ANTILLEAN

This is a great dressing-up cardigan. The idea is very simple: Knit the body of the cardigan in one yarn and the sleeves in a contrasting one. I have used a nylon yarn threaded with sequins for the sleeves—when photographed at dusk, as this was, you can really see all those sequins glinting. This is the ideal design to use to experiment with yarn and color combinations: you can work tone-on-tone or in hedonistic color clash.

TO FIT DRESS SIZE:

8	10	12	14	16	18	**US**
10	12	14	16	18	20	**UK**
38	40	42	44	46	48	**EU**

ACTUAL SIZE: Ease allowance approx 5 cm (2 in)

86	90	96	102	106	112	cm
34	35 ½	37 ¾	40 ¼	41 ¾	44	in

FINISHED LENGTH:

45.5	45.5	48.5	48.5	51	51	cm
18	18	19	19	20	20	in

SLEEVE LENGTH:

45.5	45.5	48.5	48.5	51	51	cm
18	18	19	19	20	20	in

YARN

Main body knitted in worsted-weight yarn
2nd size photographed in Nautical Cotton and Coquette
A. Nautical Cotton sh. 6 Lime

6	6	7	7	8	8	x 50g balls

B. Coquette sh. 5 Olive

6	6	7	7	8	8	x 25g balls

NEEDLES

Pair of 4 mm (US 6) needles
Pair of 4.5 mm (US 7) knitting needles

BUTTONS

1 medium mother of pearl

TENSION/GAUGE

20 sts x 28 rows to 10cm /4in square measured over st st using 4.5 mm (US 7) knitting needles using yarn A.
22 sts x 30 rows to 10cm /4in square measured over st st using 4 mm (US 6) knitting needles using yarn B.

BACK

Using 4 mm (US 6) needles and yarn A cast on 86(90, 96, 102, 106, 112) sts.
Work 20 rows in garter st.
Change to 4.5 mm (US 7) needles and beg with a K row work in st st until work measures 27.5(27.5, 29.5, 29.5, 31, 31) cm **(11(11, 11½, 11½, 12, 12)in)** from cast-on edge, ending with RS facing for next row.

SHAPE ARMHOLES

Cast off 4(5, 6, 8, 9, 10) sts at beg next 2 rows and 3(3, 4, 4, 4, 5) sts at beg foll 2 rows. (72(74, 76, 78, 80, 82) sts)
Dec 1 st at both ends of next row and 3 foll alt rows.
(64(66, 68, 70, 72, 74) sts)
Work without further shaping until work measures 18(18, 19, 19, 20, 20) cm **(7(7, 7½, 7½, 8, 8)in)** from armhole, ending with RS facing for next row.

SHAPE SHOULDERS AND BACK NECK

Cast off 5(5, 5, 6, 6, 6) sts at the beg next 2 rows.
Cast off 5(5, 5, 6, 6, 6) sts beg next row, K until 7(8, 9, 8, 9, 10) sts remain on needle, turn, leave rem sts on a holder.
Cast off 3 sts, P to end.
Cast off rem 4(5, 6, 5, 6, 7) sts.
Rejoin yarn to rem sts, cast off center 30 sts, work to end.
Complete to match first side, reversing shapings.

LEFT FRONT

Using 4 mm (US 6) needles and yarn A cast on 43(45, 48, 51, 53, 56) sts.
Work 20 rows in garter st.
Change to 4.5 mm (US 7) needles.
Next row (RS): Knit.
Next row: K10, P to end.
These 2 rows form the garter st edging at front edge and are rep throughout.
Cont in patt until work measures 27.5(27.5, 29.5, 29.5, 31:31) cm **(11(11, 11½, 11½, 12, 12)in)** from cast-on edge, ending with RS facing for next row.

SHAPE ARMHOLE

Cast off 4(5, 6, 8, 9, 10) sts at beg next row and 3(3, 4, 4, 4, 5) sts at beg foll alt row. (36(37, 38, 39, 40, 41)sts)
Work 1 row.
Dec 1 st at armhole edge on next row and 3 foll alt rows.
(32(33, 34, 35, 36, 37)sts)
Work without further shaping until front is 11 rows shorter than back to shoulder shaping, ending with **WS** facing for next row.
Next row (WS): K10, leave these on a holder, P to end.
Work 1 row.
Next row (WS): Cast off 4 sts, P to end.
(18(19, 20, 21, 22, 23)sts)
Dec 1 st at neck edge on next 4 rows.
(14(15, 16, 17, 18, 19) sts)

Work without further shaping until front matches back to shoulder, ending with RS facing for next row.

SHAPE SHOULDER

Cast off 5(5, 5, 6, 6, 6) sts at the beg next row and foll alt row.
Work 1 row.
Cast off rem 4(5, 6, 5, 6, 7) sts.

RIGHT FRONT

Using 4 mm (US 6) needles and yarn A cast on 43(45, 48, 51, 53, 56) sts.
Work 20 rows in garter st.
Change to 4.5 mm (US 7) needles.
Next row (RS): Knit.
Next row: P to last 10 sts, K10.
These 2 rows form the garter st edging at front edge and are rep throughout.
Complete to match left front, reversing shapings and working an extra row before beg armhole, neck, and shoulder shaping.

SLEEVES (work both the same)

Using 4 mm (US 10) needles and yarn A cast on 126 sts.
Work 2 rows in garter st.
Next row (RS) (dec): (K2tog, K1) to end. (84 sts)
Next row: Purl.
Change to yarn B and beg with a K row work 16 rows in st st, ending with RS facing for next row.
Dec 1 st at each end of next row and every foll 4th row until 60 sts rem.
Work until sleeve measures 30.5 cm **(12 in)**, ending with RS facing for next row.
Inc 1 st at each end of next row and every foll 6th row until there are 66(66, 70, 70, 74, 74) sts.
Work without further shaping until sleeve measures 45.5(45.5, 48.5, 48.5, 51, 51) cm **(18(18, 19, 19, 20, 20)in)**, ending with RS facing for next row.

SHAPE SLEEVEHEAD

Cast off 5(5, 6, 6, 7, 7) sts at beg next 2 rows, and 3 sts at beg foll 2 rows. (50(50, 52, 52, 54, 54) sts)
Dec 1 st at each end of next 3 rows and 4 foll alt rows.
(36(36, 38, 38, 40, 40) sts)
Work 3 rows.
Dec 1 st at each end of next row and 3 foll 4th rows.
(28(28, 30, 30, 32, 32) sts)
Work 1 row.
Dec 1 st at each end of next row and 2 foll alt rows, then at each end of foll row. (20(20, 22, 22, 24, 24)sts)
Cast off 3 sts at beg next 4 rows.
Cast off rem 8(8, 10, 10, 12, 12) sts.

MAKING UP

Press/block as described in finishing techniques (pg 158).
Join both shoulder seams using back stitch.

NECK EDGING

With RS of right front facing and using 4 mm (US 6)
needles and yarn A, K across 10 sts left on holder, pick
up and K15 sts to shoulder, 36 sts across back neck and
15 sts down left front neck to sts on holder, K10. (86 sts)
Work 2 rows in garter st.
Cast off Kwise on **WS**.
Join side and sleeve seams.
Place center of cast-off edge of sleeve to shoulder
seam. Set in sleeve, easing sleevehead into armhole.

MAKE BUTTON LOOP

Use 1 strand of yarn A and make a 5 cm **(2 in)** length of
chain cording—with a slip knot in right hand, *pull yarn
through to make a new slip knot, rep from * until chain is
the reqired length. This takes a little practice to get

an even tension.
Sew button loop into place at start of neck shaping
on right front.
Sew on button to correspond with button loop.

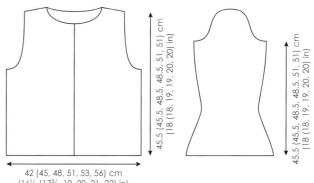

42 (45, 48, 51, 53, 56) cm
(16½ (17¾, 19, 20, 21, 22) in)

45.5 (45.5, 48.5, 48.5, 51, 51) cm
(18 (18, 19, 19, 20, 20) in)

VIOLA

The inspiration for this design comes from the lagoons of Venice. I used Glisten to cast on the garment, to give the edging a shimmer and Kashmir Aran for the body of the design. The rib is inspired by the pointed towers of the churches seen in the background. The sailor collar, an homage to the gondoliers, is worked at the same time as the fronts.

TO FIT DRESS SIZE:

8	10	12	14	16	18	**US**
10	12	14	16	18	20	**UK**
38	40	42	44	46	48	**EU**

ACTUAL SIZE: Ease allowance approx 5 cm (2 in)

86	91	97	102	107	112	cm
34	36	38	40	42	44	in

FINISHED LENGTH:

48.5	48.5	51	51	53.5	53.5	cm
19	19	20	20	21	21	in

SLEEVE LENGTH:

45.5	45.5	48.5	48.5	51	51	cm
18	18	19	19	20	20	in

YARN

Knitted in aran-weight yarn
2nd size photographed in Louisa Harding Glisten and Kashmir Aran
A. Glisten Sh. 3 Pale Blue

1	1	1	1	1	1	x 50g balls

B. Kashmir Aran Sh. 23 Lagoon

11	11	12	13	14	14	x 50g balls

NEEDLES

Pair of 4 mm (US 6) knitting needles
Pair of 5 mm (US 8) knitting needles

BUTTONS

12 small mother of pearl

TENSION/GAUGE

18 sts x 24 rows to 10cm (4 in) square measured over st st using 5 mm (US 8) knitting needles

NOTE

The chart for this pattern is shown for multiple sizes; do not work any incomplete eyelet patterns at side edges. Take stitches into stocking stitch.

BACK

Using 4 mm (US 6) needles and yarn A, work picot cast-on as folls:
*Cast on 5 sts using the cable cast-on method, cast off 2 sts, slip st on RH needle back onto LH needle (3 sts now on LH needle), rep from * until 75(81, 87, 90, 96, 99) sts on needle, cast on 2(0, 0, 0, 1, 2) sts.
(77(81, 87, 91, 97, 101) sts.
Next row (RS): Knit.
Change to yarn B.
Next row (WS): Purl.
Beg with a RS row work 30 rows from chart beg and ending rows as indicated on chart for appropriate size.

1ST & 5TH SIZE ONLY
Work first and last st on chart as a knit st.
Change to 5 mm (US 8) needles and beg with a K row work in st st until work measures 30.5(30.5, 32, 32, 33.5, 33.5)cm **(12(12, 12½, 12½, 13, 13)in)** from cast-on edge, ending with RS facing for next row.

SHAPE ARMHOLES
Cast off 3(4, 4, 5, 5, 6) sts at beg next 2 rows and 3(3, 3, 3, 4, 4) sts at beg foll 2 rows. (65(67, 73, 75, 79, 81)sts)
Next row (RS) (dec): K3, K2tog, K to last 5 sts, K2tog tbl, K3.
Work 1 row.
Dec 1 st at each end as above on next row and 1(1, 3, 3, 4, 4) foll alt rows. (59(61, 63, 65, 67, 69)sts)

Work without further shaping until work measures 18(18, 19, 19, 20, 20)cm **(7(7, 7½, 7½, 8, 8)in)** from armhole, ending with RS facing for next row.

SHAPE SHOULDERS AND BACK NECK
Cast off 5(6, 6, 6, 6, 6) sts at beg next 4 rows.
Cast off 6(5, 5, 6, 6, 7) sts at beg next 2 rows, turn, leaving rem 27(27, 29, 29, 31, 31) sts on a holder.

LEFT FRONT

Using 4 mm (US 6) needles and yarn A, work picot cast-on as folls:
*Cast on 5 sts using the cable cast-on method, cast off 2 sts, slip st on RH needle back onto LH needle (3 sts now on LH needle), rep from * until 39(39, 42, 45, 48, 51) sts on needle, cast on 0(2, 2, 1, 1, 0) sts.
39(41, 44, 46, 49, 51) sts.
Next row (RS): Knit.
Change to yarn B.
Next row (WS): Purl.
Beg with a RS row work 30 rows from chart beg and ending rows as indicated on chart for appropriate size.

NOTE 1ST & 5TH SIZE ONLY
Work first st on chart as a knit st.
Change to 5 mm (US 8) needles and beg with a K row work in st st until work measures 30.5(30.5, 32, 32,

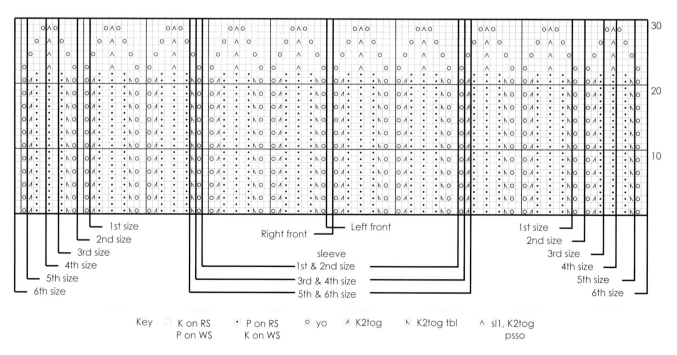

Key
- ☐ K on RS / P on WS
- • P on RS / K on WS
- ○ yo
- ⊠ K2tog
- ⊠ K2tog tbl
- ⋀ sl1, K2tog psso

Note: Do not work any incomplete eyelet patterns, work in stocking stitch

33.5, 33.5)cm **(12(12, 12½, 12½, 13, 13)in)** from cast-on edge, ending with RS facing for next row.

Shape armhole
Cast off 3(4, 4, 5, 5, 6) sts at beg next row and 3(3, 3, 3, 4, 4) sts at beg foll alt row. (33(34, 37, 38, 40, 41)sts)
Work 1 row.
Place a marker at center front edge.
Next row (RS) (dec): K3, K2tog, K to end.
Work 1 row.
Dec 1 st at armhole edge as above on next row and 1(1, 3, 3, 4, 4) foll alt rows. (30(31, 32, 33, 34, 35)sts)
Work without further shaping until work measures 18(18, 19, 19, 20, 20)cm **(7(7, 7½, 7½, 8, 8)in)** from armhole, ending with RS facing for next row.

Shape shoulder
Cast off 5(6, 6, 6, 6, 6) sts at beg next row and foll alt row.
Work 1 row.
Cast off 6(5, 5, 6, 6, 7) sts at beg next row, K to end.
Leave rem 14(14, 15, 15, 16, 16) sts on a holder.

Right Front

Using 4 mm (US 6) needles and yarn A, work picot cast-on as folls:
*Cast on 5 sts using the cable cast-on method, cast off 2 sts, slip st on RH needle back onto LH needle (3 sts now on LH needle), rep from * until 39(39, 42, 45, 48, 51) sts on needle, cast on 0(2, 2, 1, 1, 0) sts.
39(41, 44, 46, 49, 51) sts.
Next row (RS): Knit.
Change to yarn B.
Next row (WS): Purl.
Beg with a RS row work 30 rows from chart beg and ending rows as indicated on chart for appropriate size.

Note 1st & 5th size only
Work last st on chart as a knit st.
Change to 5 mm (US 8) needles and beg with a K row work in st st until work measures 30.5(30.5, 32, 32, 33.5, 33.5)cm **(12(12, 12½, 12½, 13, 13)in)** from cast-on edge, ending with RS facing for next row.
Complete to match left front, reversing shapings, marker placement and working an extra row before beg armhole and shoulder shaping.

Sleeves (work both the same)

Using 4 mm (US 6) needles and yarn A, work picot cast-on as folls:
*Cast on 5 sts using the cable cast-on method, cast off 2 sts, slip st on RH needle back onto LH needle (3 sts now on LH needle), rep from * until 39(39, 42, 42, 45, 45) sts on needle, cast on 2(2, 1, 1, 0, 0) sts.
41(41, 43, 43, 45, 45) sts.

Next row (RS): Knit.
Change to yarn B.
Next row (WS): Purl.
Beg with a RS row work 30 rows from chart beg and ending rows as indicated on chart for appropriate size.

Note 3rd & 4th size only
Work first and last st on chart as a knit st.
Change to 5 mm (US 8) needles and beg with a K row cont to work in st st AT THE SAME TIME inc 1 st at each end next row and every foll 12th(12th, 10th, 10th, 10th, 10th) to 53(53, 57, 57, 61, 61) sts.
Work without further shaping until work measures 45.5(45.5, 48.5, 48.5, 51, 51) cm **(18(18, 19, 19, 20, 20)in)** from cast on, ending with RS facing for next row.

Shape sleevehead
Cast off 4 sts at beg next 2 rows. (45(45, 49, 49, 53, 53) sts)
Dec 1 st at each end of next 3 rows and 2 foll alt rows. (35(35, 39, 39, 43, 43) sts)
Work 3 rows.
Dec 1 st at each end of next row and 3 foll 4th rows. (27(27, 31, 31, 35, 35) sts)
Work 1 row.
Dec 1 st at each end of next row and foll alt row, then on foll row. (21(21, 25, 25, 29, 29) sts)
Cast off 3 sts beg next 4 rows.
Cast off rem 9(9, 13, 13, 17, 17) sts.

Making up

Press/block as described in finishing techniques (pg 158). Join both shoulder seams.

Sailor collar
With RS facing and using 5 mm (US 8) needles, rejoin yarn B to sts on holder at right front, knit across 14(14, 15, 15, 16, 16) sts from holder, K27(27, 29, 29, 31, 31) sts across holder at back neck, then K across 14(14, 15, 15, 16, 16) sts from holder at left front. (55(55, 59, 59, 63, 63) sts)
Beg with a P row work 12.5 cm **(5 in)** in st st ending with **WS** of work, RS of sailor collar, facing for next row.
Change to 4 mm (US 6) needles and yarn A.
Work 4 rows in garter st.
Work picot cast-off as folls:
Cast off 3 sts, *slip st on RH needle back onto LH needle, cast on 2 sts, then cast off 5 sts, rep from * to end.

Right front band
With RS of right front facing and using 4 mm (US 6) needles and yarn A pick up and K 62(62, 64, 64, 66, 66) sts up right front to marker.
Work 2 rows in garter st.
Cast off Kwise on **WS**, making button loops as folls:
Cast off 2 sts, * **make button loop:** using last cast-off st make a chain of 4 sts—using the last st cast off—1 st on RH needle, (insert LH needle into this st, knit the

stitch—1 st on RH needle) 4 times—chain made, 1 st on RH needle. Pick up last cast off st with LH needle, knit this st again, take last st of chain over this st, (button loop made), cast off 4 sts. Work from * 11 times, **make button loop**, cast off rem sts.

Left front band

With RS of left front facing and using 4 mm (US 6) needles and yarn A, starting at marker on left front
pick up K 62(62, 64, 64, 66, 66) sts down left front to cast-on edge.
Work 2 rows in garter st.
Cast off Kwise on **WS**.

Right side sailor collar edging

With RS of collar facing, **WS** of work, using 4 mm (US 6) needles and yarn A, start at cast-off edge of sailor collar pick up and K 62 sts to marker.

Knit 3 rows.
Work picot cast-off as folls:
Cast off 3 sts, *slip st on RH needle back onto LH needle, cast on 2 sts, then cast off 5 sts, rep from * to end.

Left side sailor collar edging

With RS of collar facing, **WS** of work, using 4 mm (US 6) needles and yarn A, starting at front neck marker pick up and K62 sts to cast off edge of sailor collar.
Knit 3 rows.
Work picot cast-off as folls:
Cast off 3 sts, *slip st on RH needle back onto LH needle, cast on 2 sts, then cast off 5 sts, rep from * to end.
Join side and sleeve seams.
Place center of cast-off edge of sleeve to shoulder seam. Set in sleeve, easing sleevehead into armhole.
Sew on buttons to correspond with button loops.

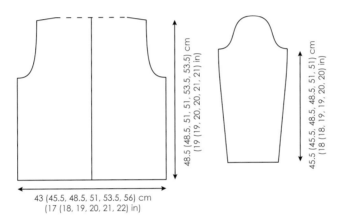

48.5 (48.5, 51, 51, 53.5, 53.5) cm
(19 (19, 20, 20, 21, 21) in)

45.5 (45.5, 48.5, 48.5, 51, 51) cm
(18 (18, 19, 19, 20, 20) in)

43 (45.5, 48.5, 51, 53.5, 56) cm
(17 (18, 19, 20, 21, 22) in)

CONTARINI

This design is from my Venezia collection and was inspired by the Ca' d'Oro, or House of Gold. Contarini is the name of the family who commissioned the building, built in the fifteenth century and fully gilded with gold leaf. The pattern for the Fair Isle border was inspired by the stone work, and the combination of gray and coral mimics the color of the marble after centuries of bleaching sun and lashing storms have worn away the gold. The building remains as magnificent and enchanting today, true to its opulent origins.

To fit dress size:

8	10	12	14	16	18	**US**
10	12	14	16	18	20	**UK**
38	40	42	44	46	48	**EU**

Actual size: Ease allowance approx 5 cm (2 in)

86	90	97	103	106	110	cm
34	35½	38¼	40½	41¾	43¼	in

Finished length:

48.5	48.5	51	51	53.5	53.5	cm
19	19	20	20	21	21	in

Sleeve length:

37	37	39.5	39.5	42	42	cm
14½	14½	15½	15½	16½	16½	in

Yarn

Knitted in double knitting–weight yarn
1st size photographed in Louisa Harding Kimono Angora Pure
A. sh. 10 Coral

1	1	1	1	2	2	x 25g balls

B. sh. 12 Dove

6	6	6	7	7	7	x 25g balls

Needles

Pair of 3.25 mm (US 3) knitting needles
Pair of 4 mm (US 6) knitting needles
Pair of 4.5 mm (US 7) knitting needles

Ribbon

2 meters (79 in) x 6 mm (¼ in) wide ribbon

Tension/gauge

22 sts x 30 rows to 10cm (4 in) square measured over Fair Isle patt using 4.5 mm (US 7) knitting needles
22 sts x 30 rows to 10cm (4 in) square measured over st st using 4 mm (US 6) knitting needles

BACK

Using 3.25 mm (US 3) needles and yarn A work picot cast-on as folls:
*Cast on 5 sts using the cable cast-on method, cast off 2 sts, slip st on RH needle back onto LH needle (3 sts now on LH needle), rep from * until 93(99, 105, 111, 117, 120) sts on needle, cast on 2(0, 2, 2, 0, 1) sts.
(95(99, 107, 113, 117, 121) sts)
Work 2 rows in garter st.
Change to yarn B and work eyelet edging as folls:
Work 5 rows in garter st.
Next row (WS): P1, (yo, P2tog) to end.
Work 4 rows in garter st.
Change to 4 mm (US 6) needles and yarn A.
Next row (RS): Knit.
Change to yarn B and beg with a P row work 3 rows in st st.
Change to 4.5 mm (US 7) needles and, joining in and breaking off yarn as required, work Fair Isle pattern from chart beg and ending rows as indicated on chart for appropriate size to chart row 11.
Change to 4 mm (US 6) needles and yarn B and beg with a P row work 3 rows in st st.
Change to yarn A.
Next row (RS): Knit.
Change to yarn B.
Next row (WS): Purl.
Purl 4 rows.
Next row (RS): K1, (yo, K2tog) to end.
Purl 4 rows.
Change to yarn A.
Next row (WS): Purl.
Change to yarn B and beg with a K row cont to work in st st only.
Cont in st st until work measures 30.5(30.5, 32, 32, 33.5, 33.5)cm **(12(12, 12½, 12½, 13, 13)in)** from cast-on edge, ending with RS facing for next row.

SHAPE ARMHOLES

Cast off 4(5, 7, 8, 9, 10) sts at beg next 2 rows and 3(3, 3, 4, 4, 4) sts at beg 2 foll rows.
(81(83, 87, 89, 91, 93) sts)
Dec 1 st at each end of next row and 3(3, 4, 4, 4, 4) foll alt rows.

(73(75, 77, 79, 81, 83) sts)
Work without further shaping until work measures 18(18, 19, 19, 20, 20) cm **(7(7, 7½, 7½, 8, 8)in)** from armhole, ending with RS facing for next row.

SHAPE SHOULDERS AND BACK NECK

Cast off 7(7, 7, 7, 7, 8) sts at beg next 2 rows.
Cast off 7(7, 7, 7, 7, 8) sts, K until 9(10, 10, 11, 11, 10) sts on needle, turn, leave rem sts on a holder.
Cast off 3 sts, P to end.
Cast off rem 6(7, 7, 8, 8, 7) sts.
Rejoin yarn to rem sts, cast off center 27(27, 29, 29, 31, 31) sts, K to end.
Complete to match first side, reversing shapings.

LEFT FRONT

Using 3.25 mm (US 3) needles and yarn A work picot cast-on as folls:
*Cast on 5 sts using the cable cast-on method, cast off 2 sts, slip st on RH needle back onto LH needle (3 sts now on LH needle), rep from * until 48(48, 54, 57, 57, 60) sts on needle, cast on 0(2, 0, 0, 2, 1) sts.
(48(50, 54, 57, 59, 61) sts)
Work 2 rows in garter st.
Change to yarn B and work eyelet edging as folls:
Work 5 rows in garter st.
Next row (WS): P2(2, 2, 1, 1, 1), (yo, P2tog) to end.
Work 4 rows in garter st.
Change to 4 mm (US 6) needles and yarn A.
Next row (RS): Knit.
Change to yarn B and beg with a P row work 3 rows in st st.
Change to 4.5 mm (US 7) needles and, joining in and breaking off yarn as required, work Fair Isle pattern from chart beg and ending rows as indicated on chart for appropriate size to chart row 11.
Change to 4 mm (US 6) needles and yarn B and beg with a P row work 3 rows in st st.
Change to yarn A.
Next row (RS): Knit.
Change to yarn B.
Next row (WS): Purl.
Purl 4 rows.

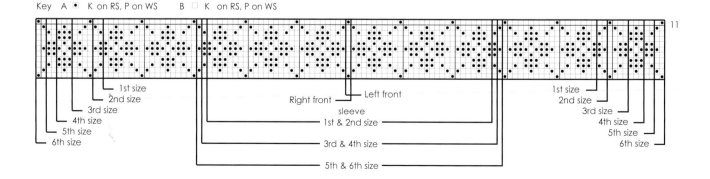

Next row (RS): K2(2, 2, 1, 1, 1), (yo, K2tog) to end.
Purl 4 rows.
Change to yarn A.
Next row (WS): Purl.
Change to yarn B and beg with a K row cont to work in st st only.
Cont in st st until work measures 30.5(30.5, 32, 32, 33.5, 33.5)cm **(12(12, 12½, 12½, 13, 13)in)** from cast-on edge, ending with RS facing for next row.

Shape armhole

Cast off 4(5, 7, 8, 9, 10) sts at beg next row and 3(3, 3, 4, 4, 4) sts at beg foll alt row.
(41(42, 44, 45, 46, 47) sts)
Work 1 row.
Dec 1 st at armhole edge on next row and 3(3, 4, 4, 4, 4) foll alt rows.
(37(38, 39, 40, 41, 42) sts)
Work without further shaping until work is 11 rows shorter than back to shoulder shaping, ending with **WS** facing for next row.

Shape front neck

Cast off 10(10, 11, 11, 12, 12) sts at beg next row and 3 sts at beg foll alt row. (24(25, 25, 26, 26, 27) sts)
Dec 1 st at neck edge on next 4 rows.
(20(21, 21, 22, 22, 23) sts)
Work until front matches back to shoulder, ending with RS facing for next row.

Shape shoulder

Cast off 7(7, 7, 7, 7, 8) sts beg next row and foll alt row.
Work 1 row.
Cast off rem 6(7, 7, 8, 8, 7) sts.

Right front

Using 3.25 mm (US 3) needles and yarn A work picot cast-on as folls:
*Cast on 5 sts using the cable cast-on method, cast off 2 sts, slip st on RH needle back onto LH needle (3 sts now on LH needle), rep from * until 48(48, 54, 57, 57, 60) sts on needle, cast on 0(2, 0, 0, 2, 1) sts.
(48(50, 54, 57, 59, 61) sts)
Work 2 rows in garter st.
Change to yarn B and work eyelet edging as folls:
Work 5 rows in garter st.
Next row (WS): P2(2, 2, 1, 1, 1), (yo, P2tog) to end.
Work 4 rows in garter st.
Change to 4 mm (US 6) needles and yarn A.
Next row (RS): Knit.
Change to yarn B and beg with a P row work 3 rows in st st.
Change to 4.5 mm (US 7) needles and, joining in and breaking off yarn as required, work Fair Isle pattern from chart beg and ending rows as indicated on chart for appropriate size to chart row 11.
Change to 4 mm (US 6) needles and yarn B and beg

with a P row work 3 rows in st st.
Change to yarn A.
Next row (RS): Knit.
Change to yarn B.
Next row (WS): Purl.
Purl 4 rows.
Next row (RS): K2(2, 2, 1, 1, 1), (yo, K2tog) to end.
Purl 4 rows.
Change to yarn A.
Next row (WS): Purl.
Change to yarn B and beg with a K row cont to work in st st only.
Complete to match left front, reversing shapings and working an extra row before working armhole, neck, and shoulder shaping.

Sleeves (work both the same)

Using 3.25 mm (US 3) needles and yarn A, work picot cast-on as folls:
*Cast on 5 sts using the cable cast-on method, cast off 2 sts, slip st on RH needle back onto LH needle (3 sts now on LH needle), rep from * until 54(54, 57, 57, 57, 57) sts on needle, cast on 1(1, 0, 0, 2, 2) sts. (55(55, 5, 57, 59, 59) sts)
Work 2 rows in garter st.
Change to yarn B and work eyelet edging as folls:
Work 5 rows in garter st.
Next row (WS): P1, (yo, P2tog) to end.
Work 4 rows in garter st.
Change to 4 mm (US 6) needles and yarn A.
Next row (RS): Knit.
Change to yarn B and beg with a P row work 3 rows in st st.
Change to 4.5 mm (US 7) needles and, joining in and breaking off yarn as required, work Fair Isle pattern from chart beg and ending rows as indicated on chart for appropriate size to chart row 11.
Change to 4 mm (US 6) needles and yarn B and beg with a P row work 3 rows in st st.
Change to yarn A.
Next row (RS): Knit.
Change to yarn B.
Next row (WS): Purl.
Purl 4 rows.
Next row (RS): K1, (yo, K2tog) to end.
Purl 4 rows.
Change to yarn A.
Next row (WS): Purl.
Change to yarn B and beg with a K row work 4 rows in st st ending with RS facing for next row.
Inc 1 st at each end of next row and every foll 6th row to 71(71, 75, 75, 79, 79) sts.
Work without further shaping until work measures 37(37, 39.5, 39.5, 42, 42)cm **(14½(14½, 15½, 15½, 16½, 16½)in)** from cast-on edge, ending with RS facing for next row.

SHAPE SLEEVEHEAD

Cast off 4 sts at beg next 2 rows and 3 sts at beg 2 foll rows. (57(57, 61, 61, 65, 65) sts)
Dec 1 st at each end of next 3 rows and 3 foll alt rows. (45, 45, 49, 49, 53, 53) sts)
Work 3 rows.
Dec 1 st at each end of next row and 2 foll 4th rows. (39(39, 43, 43, 47, 47) sts)
Work 1 row.
Dec 1 st at each end of next row and 4 foll alt rows, then on every foll row until 23(23, 27, 27, 31, 31) sts rem, ending with RS facing for next row.
Cast off 3 sts beg next 4 rows.
Cast off rem 11(11, 15, 15, 19, 19) sts.

MAKING UP

Press/block as described in finishing techniques (pg 158).
Join both shoulder seams using back stitch.

BUTTONHOLE BAND

With RS of right front facing and using 3.25 mm (US 3) needles and yarn B, pick up and K97(97, 103, 103, 109, 109) sts up right front to neck.
Work 2 rows in garter st.
Next row (WS): P1, (yo, P2tog) to end.
Work 3 rows in garter st.
Cast off Kwise on **WS**.

BUTTONBAND

With RS of left front facing and using 3.25 mm (US 3) needles and yarn B, pick up and K 97(97, 103, 103, 109, 109) sts down left front.
Work 2 rows in garter st.
Next row (WS): P1, (yo, P2tog) to end.
Work 3 rows in garter st.
Cast off Kwise on **WS**.

NECK BAND

With RS facing of right front and using 3.25 mm (US 3) needles and yarn B, pick up and K 3 sts from front band and 23(23, 26, 26, 29, 29) sts up right front neck to shoulder, 33(33, 35, 35, 37, 37) sts across back neck and 23(23, 26, 26, 29, 29) sts down left front neck, and 3 sts from front band. (85(85, 93, 93, 101, 101) sts)
Work 2 rows in garter st.
Next row (WS): P1, (yo, P2tog) to end.
Work 3 rows in garter st.
Cast off Kwise on **WS**.
Join side and sleeve seams.
Place center of cast-off edge of sleeve to shoulder seam. Set in sleeve, easing sleevehead into armhole.
Sew side and sleeve seams

FINISHING

Using photograph as a guide insert ribbons as follows:
Cut 1 meter (39½ in) length of ribbon, starting at right front opening thread ribbon through center eyelet patt, thread across back and left front to left front opening.
Cut 50 cm (39 ½ in) length of ribbon, starting at center of sleeve, thread ribbon around the bottom eyelet patt on sleeve bringing it back to the start. Tie in a bow.
Repeat for the opposite side. ∼

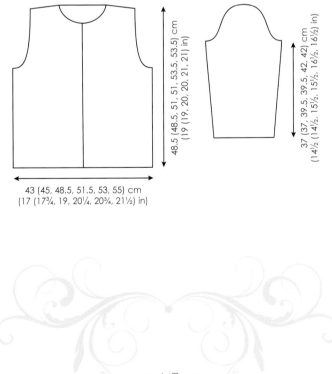

43 (45, 48.5, 51.5, 53, 55) cm
(17 (17¾, 19, 20¼, 20¾, 21½) in)

48.5 (48.5, 51, 51, 53.5, 53.5) cm
(19 (19, 20, 20, 21, 21) in)

37 (37, 39.5, 39.5, 42, 42) cm
(14½ (14½, 15½, 15½, 16½, 16½) in)

SOFIA

This elegant evening bolero, photographed at dusk on the banks of the lagoon in Venice, is the ultimate dressing-up garment. Knitted in a midnight-blue shade of Glisten, it flatterers the figure and shimmers in the fading light. Add a pair of jeans and a tee and you have a very sophisticated, "dressed up / dressed down" ensemble.

TO FIT DRESS SIZE:

8	10	12	14	16	18	**US**
10	12	14	16	18	20	**UK**
38	40	42	44	46	48	**EU**

ACTUAL SIZE: Ease allowance approx 5 cm (2 in)

87	91	97	103	107	111	cm
34	36	38	40 ½	42	44	in

FINISHED LENGTH:

38	38	40.5	40.5	43	43	cm
15	15	16	16	17	17	in

YARN

Knitted in worsted-weight yarn
1st size photographed in Louisa Harding sh. 27 Murano

6	6	7	7	8	8	x 50g balls

NEEDLES

Pair of 4.5 mm (US 7) knitting needles
Pair of 5 mm (US 8) knitting needles

BUTTONS

5 small mother of pearl

TENSION/GAUGE

20 sts x 28 rows to 10cm (4 in) square measured over st st using 5 mm (US 8) knitting needles

BACK

Using 5 mm (US 8) needles cast on 81(85, 91, 97, 101, 105) sts.
Beg with a K row work 8 rows in st st, ending with RS facing for next row.
Next row (RS) (inc): K3, M1, K to last 3 sts, M1, K3.
(83(87, 93, 99, 103, 107) sts)
Beg with a P row work 7 rows in st st, ending with RS facing for next row.
Inc 1 st at each end as above on next row and foll 8th row. (87(91, 97, 103, 107, 111) sts)
Cont in st st until work measures 14(14, 15.5, 15.5, 17, 17) cm **(5½(5½, 6, 6, 6½, 6½ in)** from cast-on edge ending with RS facing for next row.

SHAPE ARMHOLES

Cast off 4(5, 7, 8, 9, 10) sts at beg next 2 rows and 3(3, 3, 4, 4, 4) sts at beg 2 foll rows. (73(75, 77, 79, 81, 83) sts)
Dec 1 st at both ends of next row and 3 foll alt rows. (65(67, 69, 71, 73, 75) sts)
Work without further shaping until work measures 18(18, 19, 19, 20, 20) cm **(7(7, 7½, 7½, 8, 8)in)** from armhole, ending with RS facing for next row.

SHAPE SHOULDERS AND BACK NECK

Cast off 5(6, 6, 6, 6, 6) sts at beg next 2 rows.
Cast off 5(6, 6, 6, 6, 6) sts, K until 9(8, 8, 9, 9, 10) sts on needle, turn, leave rem sts on a holder.
Cast off 3 sts, P to end.
Cast off rem 6(5, 5, 6, 6, 7) sts.
Rejoin yarn to rem sts, cast off center 27(27, 29, 29, 31, 31) sts, K to end.
Complete to match first side, reversing shapings.

LEFT FRONT

Using 5 mm (US 8) needles cast on 25(27, 30, 33, 35, 37) sts.
Row 1 (RS): Knit.
Row 2 (inc): P1, M1, P to end. (26(28, 31, 34, 36, 38) sts)
Row 3 (inc): K to last st, M1, K1. (27(29, 32, 35, 37, 39) sts)
Row 4 (inc): P1, M1, P to end. (28(30, 33, 36, 38, 40) sts)
Row 5 (inc): K to last st, M1, K1. (29(31, 34, 37, 39, 41) sts)
Row 6: Purl.
Row 7 (inc): K to last st, M1, K1. (30(32, 35, 38, 40, 42) sts)
Row 8: Purl.
Row 9 (inc): K3, M1, K to last st, M1, K1.
(32(34, 37, 40, 42, 44) sts)
Row 10: Purl.
Row 11 (inc): K to last st, M1, K1. (33(35, 38, 41, 43, 45) sts)
Row 12: Purl.
Row 13 (inc): K to last st, M1, K1. (34(36, 39, 42, 44, 46) sts)
Row 14: Purl.
Row 15 (inc): K to last st, M1, K1. (35(37, 40, 43, 45, 47) sts)
Row 16: Purl.
Row 17 (inc): K3, M1, K to end. (36(38, 41, 44, 46, 48) sts)
Beg with a P row work 7 rows in st st ending with RS facing for next row.

Inc 1 st internally as above at beg of next row.
(37(39, 42, 45, 47, 49 sts)
Cont without further shaping until work measures 14(14, 15.5, 15.5, 17, 17) cm **(5½(5½, 6, 6, 6½, 6½ in)** from cast-on edge ending with RS facing for next row.

SHAPE ARMHOLE

Cast off 4(5, 7, 8, 9, 10) sts at beg next row and 3(3, 3, 4, 4, 4) sts beg foll alt row. (30(31, 32, 33, 34, 35) sts)
Work 1 row.
Next row (RS) (dec): K3, K2tog, K to end.
(29(30, 31, 32, 33, 34) sts)
Work 1 row.
Dec at armhole edge as above on next row and 2 foll alt rows. (26(27, 28, 29, 30, 31) sts)
Work 4 rows ending with **WS** facing for next row.

SHAPE FRONT NECK

Cast off 5(5, 6, 6, 7, 7) sts at beg next row.
(21(22, 22, 23, 23, 24) sts)
Dec 1 st at neck edge on next 3 rows and 2 foll alt rows.
(16(17, 17, 18, 18, 19) sts)
Work without further shaping until work measures 18(18, 19, 19, 20, 20) cm **(7(7, 7½, 7½, 8, 8)in)** from armhole, ending with RS facing for next row.

SHAPE SHOULDER

Cast off 5(6, 6, 6, 6, 6) sts at beg next row and foll alt row.
Work 1 row.
Cast off rem 6(5, 5, 6, 6, 7) sts.

RIGHT FRONT

Using 5 mm (US 8) needles cast on 25(27, 30, 33, 35, 37) sts.
Row 1 (RS): Knit.
Row 2 (inc): P to last st, M1, P1. (26(28, 31, 34, 36, 38) sts)
Row 3 (inc): K1, M1, K to end. (27(29, 32, 35, 37, 39) sts)
Row 4 (inc): P to last st, M1, P1. (28(30, 33, 36, 38, 40) sts)
Row 5 (inc): K1, M1, K to end. (29(31, 34, 37, 39, 41) sts)
Row 6: Purl.
Row 7 (inc): K1, M1, K to end. (30(32, 35, 38, 40, 42) sts)
Row 8: Purl.
Row 9 (inc): K1, M1, K to last 3 sts M1, K3.
(32(34, 37, 40, 42, 44) sts)
Row 10: Purl.
Row 11 (inc): K1, M1, K to end. (33(35, 38, 41, 43, 45) sts)
Row 12: Purl.
Row 13 (inc): K1, M1, K to end. (34(36, 39, 42, 44, 46) sts)
Row 14: Purl.
Row 15 (inc): K1, M1, K to end. (35(37, 40, 43, 45, 47) sts)
Row 16: Purl.
Row 17 (inc): K to last 3 sts, M1, K3.
(36(38, 41, 44, 46, 48) sts)
Beg with a P row work 7 rows in st st ending with RS facing for next row.
Inc 1 st at end of next row as above.
(37(39, 42, 45, 47, 49 sts)

Cont without further shaping until work measures 14(14, 15.5, 15.5, 17, 17) cm **(5½(5½, 6, 6, 6½, 6½ in)** from cast-on edge ending with **WS** facing for next row.

SHAPE ARMHOLE
Cast off 4(5, 7, 8, 9, 10) sts at beg next row and 3(3, 3, 4, 4, 4) sts beg foll alt row. (30(31, 32, 33, 34, 35) sts)
Next row (RS) (dec): K to last 5 sts, K2tog, K3.
(29(30, 31, 32, 33, 34) sts)
Work 1 row.
Dec at armhole edge as above on next row and 2 foll alt rows. (26(27, 28, 29, 30, 31) sts)
Work 5 rows ending with RS facing for next row.

SHAPE FRONT NECK
Cast off 5(5, 6, 6, 7, 7) sts at beg next row. (21(22, 22, 23, 23, 24) sts)
Dec 1 st at neck edge on next 3 rows and 2 foll alt rows. (16(17, 17, 18, 18, 19) sts)
Work without further shaping until work measures 18(18, 19, 19, 20, 20) cm **(7(7, 7½, 7½, 8, 8)in)** from armhole, ending with **WS** facing for next row.

SHAPE SHOULDER
Cast off 5(6, 6, 6, 6, 6) sts at beg next row and foll alt row.
Work 1 row.
Cast off rem 6(5, 5, 6, 6, 7) sts.

CAPPED SLEEVE

Using 4.5 mm (US 7) needles cast on 43(43, 47, 47, 51, 51) sts.
Work 4 rows in garter st.
Change to 5 mm needles and beg with a K row work 2(2, 4, 4, 6, 6) rows in st st ending with RS facing for next row.
Dec 1 st at each end of next row and 5 foll 4th rows. (31(31, 35, 35, 39, 39) sts)
Work 1 row.
Dec 1 st at each end of next row and 3 foll alt rows, then

on next row. 21(21, 25, 25, 29, 29) sts.
Cast off 3 sts at beg next 4 rows. (9(9, 13, 13, 17, 17) sts)
Cast off.

MAKING UP

Press/block as described in finishing techniques (pg 158).
Join both shoulder seams using back stitch.

EDGING
Using 4.5 mm (US 7) needles cast on 12 sts and work garter st and eyelet edging as follows:
Work 2 rows in garter st.
Edging row 1 (RS): K2, yo, K2tog, K8.
Edging row 2: K9, yo, K2tog, K1.
Rep these 2 rows until lace edging fits around edge of bolero starting at right front neck shaping, down right front to side seam, across back to left side seam, up left front to left front neck shaping.
Stitch into place, allowing ease around front shaping.

NECK BAND
With RS facing of right front and using 4.5 mm (US 7) needles, pick up and K 11 sts from edging, K34(34, 35, 35, 36, 36) sts to shoulder, 33(33, 35, 35, 37, 37) sts across back neck and 34(34, 35, 35, 36, 36) sts down left front neck to edging, pick up and K 11 from edging.
(123(123, 127, 127, 131, 131) sts)
Work 2 rows in garter st.
Work picot cast-off on **WS** as folls:
Cast off 3 sts, *slip st on RH needle back onto LH needle, cast on 2 sts, then cast off 5 sts, rep from * to end.
Sew in capped sleeve as folls: Place center of cast-off edge of sleeve to shoulder seam. Set in sleevehead, easing into armhole between end of armhole shaping on back and front.
Sew on buttons to left front band as illustrated in photograph at center front. Use eyelets at center front on right front band as buttonholes.

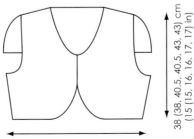

43 (45.5, 48.5, 51.5, 53.5, 55.5) cm
(17 (18, 19, 20¼, 21, 22) in)

38 (38, 40.5, 40.5, 43, 43) cm
(15 (15, 16, 16, 17, 17) in)

BUNDI

This design is taken from my collection inspired by my travels to Rajasthan in India. It's a very simple (and quick to knit) open V-neck shape, but it's the embellishment that transforms it into a textile heritage piece. Embroidery has been used for centuries to embellish knitwear; here I have used paisley shapes and then sewn beads to enhance the pattern. I have also sewn beads to each picot of the edging, adding the finishing touch.

TO FIT DRESS SIZE:

8	10	12	14	16	18	**US**
10	12	14	16	18	20	**UK**
38	40	42	44	46	48	**EU**

ACTUAL SIZE: Ease allowance approx 5 cm (2 in)

85	91	97	103	106	112	cm
33½	36	38¼	40½	41¾	44	in

FINISHED LENGTH:

45	45	46	46	47	47	cm
17¾	17¾	18	18	18½	18½	in

SLEEVE LENGTH:

30	30	32	32	34	34	cm
11¾	11¾	12¾	12¾	13½	13½	in

YARN

Knitted in bulky-weight yarn
2nd size photographed in Louisa Harding Thalia sh. 1 Thunder

5	5	6	6	7	7	x 50g hanks

NEEDLES

Pair of 7 mm (US 10½) knitting needles
Pair of 8 mm (US 11) knitting needles
7 mm (US 10½) circular needle

EXTRAS

Oddments of yarn for embroidery
Assortment of beads for embroidery

TENSION/GAUGE

13 sts x 17 rows to 10 cm (4 in) square measured over st st using 8 mm (US 11) knitting needles.

Back

Using 8 mm (US 11) needles cast on 49(53, 57, 61, 63, 67) sts.
Beg with a K row work in st st for 10 rows, ending with RS facing for next row.
Next row (RS) (inc): K3, M1, K to last 3 sts, M1, K3.
Work 9 rows.
Inc 1 st as above at each end of next row and foll 10th row. (55(59, 63, 67, 69, 73) sts)
Cont without further shaping until work measures 25 cm **(10 in)**, ending with RS facing for next row.

Shape armholes

Cast off 3(4, 5, 6, 6, 6) sts at beg of next 2 rows.
(49(51, 53, 55, 57, 61) sts)
Next row (RS) (dec): K3, K2tog, K to last 5 sts, K2tog tbl, K3. (47(49, 51, 53, 55, 59) sts)
Work 1 row.
Dec 1 st as above on next row and 1(1, 2, 2, 2, 2) foll alt rows. (43(45, 45, 47, 49, 53) sts)
Cont without further shaping until armhole measures 18(18, 19, 19, 20, 20) cm **(7(7, 7½, 7½, 8, 8) in)**, ending with RS facing for next row.

Shape shoulders and back neck

Cast off 4(4, 4, 5, 5, 6) sts at beg of next 2 rows.
(35(37, 37, 37, 39, 41) sts)
Next row (RS): Cast off 4(4, 4, 5, 5, 6) sts, K until there are 7(8, 8, 7, 8, 8) sts on RH needle and turn, leaving rem sts on a holder.
Work both sides of neck separately.
Next row: Cast off 3 sts, P to end.
Cast off rem 4(5, 5, 4, 5, 5) sts.
With RS facing rejoin yarn to sts from holder, cast off center 13 sts, K to end. (11(12, 12, 12, 13, 14) sts)
Cast off 4(4, 4, 5, 5, 6) sts at beg of next row, then 3 sts at beg of foll row.
Cast off rem 4(5, 5, 4, 5, 5) sts.

Left front

Using 8 mm (US 11) needles cast on 19(21, 23, 25, 26, 28) sts.
Beg with a K row work 2 rows in st st.
Next row (RS) (inc): K to last 3 sts, M1, K3.
(20(22, 24, 26, 27, 29) sts)
Work 1 row.
Inc as above on next row and 2 foll alt rows.
(23(25, 27, 29, 30, 32) sts)
Work 1 row.
Next row (RS) (inc): K3, M1, K to last 3 sts, M1, K3.
(25(27, 29, 31, 32, 34) sts)
Work 9 rows.
Next row (RS) (inc): K3, M1, K to end.
(26(28, 30, 32, 33, 35) sts)
Work 9 rows.
Next row (RS) (inc): K3, M1, K to end.
(27(29, 31, 33, 34, 36) sts)

Cont without further shaping until work measures 25 cm **(10 in)**, ending with RS facing for next row.

Shape armhole

Cast off 3(4, 5, 6, 6, 6) sts at beg of next row.
(24(25, 26, 27, 28, 30) sts)
Work 1 row.

Shape armhole and front neck

Next row (RS) (dec): K3, K2tog, K to last 5 sts, K2tog tbl, K3. (22(23, 24, 25, 26, 28) sts)
Work 1 row.
Dec 1 st as above on next row and 1(1, 2, 2, 2, 2) foll alt rows. (18(19, 18, 19, 20, 22) sts)
Work 1 row.
Next row (RS) (dec): K to last 5 sts, K2tog tbl, K3.
(17(18, 17, 18, 19, 21) sts)
Work 1 row.
Cont to dec at neck edge only as above on next row and 4(4, 3, 3, 3, 3) foll alt rows. (12(13, 13, 14, 15, 17) sts)
Cont without further shaping until armhole measures 18(18, 19, 19, 20, 20) cm **(7(7, 7½, 7½, 8, 8) in)**, ending with RS facing for next row.

Shape shoulder

Cast off 4(4, 4, 5, 5, 6) sts at beg of next row and foll alt row.
Work 1 row.
Cast off rem 4(5, 5, 4, 5, 5) sts.

Right front

Using 8 mm (US 11) needles cast on 19(21, 23, 25, 26, 28) sts.
Beg with a K row work 2 rows in st st.
Next row (RS) (inc): K3, M1, K to end.
(20(22, 24, 26, 27, 29) sts)
Work 1 row.
Inc as above on next row and 2 foll alt rows.
(23(25, 27, 29, 30, 32) sts)
Work 1 row.
Next row (RS) (inc): K3, M1, K to last 3 sts, M1, K3.
(25(27, 29, 31, 32, 34) sts)
Work 9 rows.
Next row (RS) (inc): K to last 3 sts, M1, K3.
(26(28, 30, 32, 33, 35) sts)
Work 9 rows.
Next row (RS) (inc): K to last 3 sts, M1, K3.
(27(29, 31, 33, 34, 36) sts)
Cont without further shaping until work measures 25 cm **(10 in)**, ending with **WS** facing for next row.

Shape armhole

Cast off 3(4, 5, 6, 6, 6) sts at beg of next row.
(24(25, 26, 27, 28, 30) sts)

SHAPE ARMHOLE AND FRONT NECK
Next row (RS) (dec): K3, K2tog, K to last 5 sts, K2tog tbl, K3. (22(23, 24, 25, 26, 28) sts)
Work 1 row.
Dec 1 st as above on next row and 1(1, 2, 2, 2, 2) foll alt rows. (18(19, 18, 19, 20, 22) sts)
Work 1 row.
Next row (RS) (dec): K3, K2tog, K to end.
(17(18, 17, 18, 19, 21) sts)
Work 1 row.
Cont to dec at neck edge only as above on next row and 4(4, 3, 3, 3, 3) foll alt rows. (12(13, 13, 14, 15, 17) sts)
Cont without further shaping until armhole measures 18(18, 19, 19, 20, 20) cm **(7(7, 7½, 7½, 8, 8) in)**, ending with **WS** facing for next row.

SHAPE SHOULDER
Cast off 4(4, 4, 5, 5, 6) sts at beg of next row and foll alt row.
Work 1 row.
Cast off rem 4(5, 5, 4, 5, 5) sts.

SLEEVES (work both the same)

Using 7 mm (US 10½) needles work picot cast-on as folls:
Cast on 5 sts using the cable cast-on method, cast off 2 sts, slip st on RH needle back onto LH needle
(3 sts now on LH needle), rep from * to * until there are 33(33, 33, 33, 36, 36) sts on needle, cast on 0(0, 2, 2, 1, 1) sts. (33(33, 35, 35, 37, 37) sts)
Work 4 rows in garter st, ending with RS facing for next row.
Change to 8mm (US 11) needles and beg with a K row work 8 rows in st st, ending with RS facing for next row.
Next row (RS) (inc): K3, M1, K to last 3 sts, M1, K3.
Work 7 rows.
Inc as above on next row and 2(2, 3, 3, 3, 3) foll 8th rows. (41(41, 45, 45, 47, 47) sts)
Cont without further shaping until sleeve measures 30(30, 32, 32, 34, 34) cm **(11¾(11¾, 12¾, 12¾, 13½, 13½) in)**, ending with RS facing for next row.

SHAPE SLEEVEHEAD
Cast off 3(3, 4, 4, 4, 4) sts at beg of next 2 rows.
(35(35, 37, 37, 39, 39) sts)
Dec 1 st at each end of next 3 rows and foll alt row.
(27(27, 29, 29, 31, 31) sts)
Work 3 rows.
Dec 1 st at each end of next row and foll 4th row.
(23(23, 25, 25, 27, 27) sts)
Work 1 row.
Dec 1 st at each end of next row and foll alt row.
(19(19, 21, 21, 23, 23) sts)
Work 1 row.
Cast off 3 sts at beg of next 4 rows. (7(7, 9, 9, 11, 11) sts)
Cast off rem sts.

MAKING UP

Press/block as described in finishing techniques (pg 158). Join both shoulder seams and left side seam using back stitch.

BOLERO EDGING
With RS facing, starting at right side seam and using 7 mm (US 10½) circular needle, pick up and knit 19(21, 23, 25, 26, 28) sts along right front cast-on edge, 13 sts around curve, 26 sts up right front to start of neck shaping, 23(23, 24, 24, 25, 25) sts up right front neck to shoulder, 19 sts across back neck, 23(23, 24, 24, 25, 25) sts down left front neck to start of neck shaping, 26 sts down left front, 13 sts around curve, 19(21, 23, 25, 26, 28) sts along left front cast-on edge, then 49(53, 57, 61, 63, 67) sts across back. (230(238, 248, 256, 262, 270) sts)
Knit 1 row, ending with RS facing for next row.
Row 2 (RS) (inc): K21(23, 25, 27, 28, 30), M1, (K4, M1) twice, K to last 78(84, 90, 96, 99, 105) sts, (M1, K4) twice, M1, K70(76, 82, 88, 91, 97). (236(244, 254, 262, 268, 276) sts)
Work picot cast-off on RS as folls:
Cast off 3 sts, *slip st on RH needle back onto LH needle, cast on 2 sts, then cast off 5 sts, rep from * to end.
Join right side sleeve seams.
Place center of cast-off edge of sleeve to shoulder seam. Set in sleevehead, easing into armhole between end of armhole shaping on back and front.

FINISHING
Using photograph as a guide and yarn oddments, work paisley and lazy daisy embroidery on garment fronts and sleeves. Embellish embroidery with a selection of beads.
Attach a bead to picot points on sleeve cast-on edges and picot point cast-off edge around fronts and back. ⌁

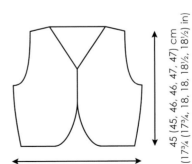

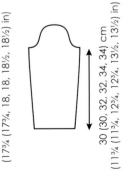

45 (45, 46, 46, 47, 47) cm
(17¾ (17¾, 18, 18, 18½, 18½) in)

42.5 (45.5, 48.5, 51.5, 53, 56) cm
(16¾ (18, 19, 20¼, 20¾, 21) in)

30 (30, 32, 32, 34, 34) cm
(11¾ (11¾, 12¾, 12¾, 13½, 13½) in)

General Information

The projects in this book have been designed to work with my very own range of yarns. I have created patterns that I hope will appeal to a wide range of knitters, from those picking up knitting needles for the first time to begin their first garment to more experienced knitters looking for that special knitwear pattern. To create interest for the knitter I have used combinations of yarns together in the same design as well as different knitted edgings, cables, picot, cast-ons, and embroidery. In this section you will find information on how to read the patterns and to finish off your project beautifully as well as information regarding different yarn types and how to substitute the suggested yarns.

THE KNITTING PATTERNS

Each pattern has written instructions; laid out as follows:

SIZES

At the beginning of each pattern, you will find a table of sizes. Each garment is designed for a specific shape—some a loose fit, some fitted close to the body. To help you decide which size to knit I have included actual widths and lengths, as well as "to fit" dress sizes and the ease allowance I suggest. Also included is a size diagram showing the shape of the garment, with the measurements for each knitted piece.

YARN

This indicates the type of yarn (e.g., worsted) and amount of yarn needed to complete the design. All of the projects that use more than one shade of yarn will include a quantity for each shade used. The quantities of yarn are based on average requirements and are therefore approximate.

NEEDLES

Listed are the suggested knitting needles to make the project. The smaller needles are usually used for edgings or ribs, the larger needles for the main fabric of the work. You might need to use different needles to achieve the gauge or tension stated in the pattern.

EXTRAS

This indicates the additional items you may require to finish your project.

TENSION/GAUGE

This is the single most important factor when you begin knitting. The fabric tension is written as, for example, 22 sts x 30 rows to 10 cm (4 in) measured over stocking stitch (stockinette stitch) using 4 mm (US 6) needles. Each pattern is worked out mathematically; If the correct tension is not achieved, the project will not fit as intended. Before embarking on knitting your project, we recommend that you check your tension as follows: Using the needle size suggested, cast on 5–10 more stitches than stated in the tension specification paragraph and work 5–10 more rows than stated. When you have knitted your tension square, lay it on a flat surface, place a rule or tape measure across it horizontally, and count the number of stitches that fall within a 10 cm (4 in) space. Place the measure vertically up the piece and count the number of rows. These figures should equal those stated in the pattern tension note. If you have too many stitches to 10 cm (4 in), try again using a larger needle; if you have too few stitches to 10 cm (4 in), use a smaller needle.

Note: Check your gauge regularly as you knit—once you become relaxed and confident with your knitting, your gauge can change.

INSTRUCTIONS

Instructions are given for the first size, with larger sizes in parentheses.
Where only one figure or instruction is given, instructions apply to all sizes.

ABBREVIATIONS

Check your chosen project as you may find a special abbreviation note. Some of the most common words used have been abbreviated as listed:

K	knit
P	purl
st(s)	stitch(es)
inc	increase(e)(ing), knit into the front and back of next st to make two stitches
dec	decreas(e)(ing), work two sts together to make one stitch
st st	stockinette stitch (right side row knit, wrong side row purl)
garter st	garter stitch (knit every row)
beg	begin(ning)
foll	follow(s)(ing)
rem	remain(ing)
rev	reverse(ing)
rep	repeat
alt	alternate
cont	continu(e)(ing)
patt	pattern
tog	together
cm	centimeter(s)
in(s)	inch(es)
RS	right side
WS	wrong side
K2tog	knit two sts together to make one stitch
tbl	through back of loop
yo	yarn over, bring yarn over needle before working next st to create an extra loop
Sl1	slip one stitch
psso	pass slipped stitch over
M1	make one stitch by picking up horizontal loop before next stitch and knitting into back of it
M1P	make one stitch by picking up horizontal loop before next stitch and purling into back of it
Kwise	Knitwise
C4(6, 8, 10)F	Slip next 2(3, 4, 5) sts onto a cable needle, hold at front of work, knit 2(3, 4, 5) sts, knit 2(3, 4, 5) sts from cable needle.
C4(6, 8, 10)B	Slip next 2(3, 4, 5) sts onto a cable needle, hold at back of work, knit 2(3, 4, 5) sts, knit 2(3, 4, 5) sts from cable needle.

USA GLOSSARY

UK	USA
Cast off	Bind off
Tension	Gauge
Stocking stitch	Stockinette stitch
Moss stitch	Seed stitch

FINISHING TECHNIQUES

Putting your project together
After spending many hours knitting, it is essential that you complete your project correctly. By following the simple written instructions, we will show you how easy it is to achieve a beautifully finished accessory.

PRESSING—For natural fibers—With the wrong side of the fabric facing, pin out each knitted piece onto an ironing board using the measurements given as a guide. As each yarn is different, refer to the ball band and press the pieces according to the instructions given. Pressing the knitted fabric will help the pieces maintain their shape and give a smooth finish.

BLOCKING— For synthetic fibers—With the wrong side of the fabric facing, pin out each knitted piece onto blocking or ironing board using the measurements given as a guide. Cover each piece with a cloth (e.g., tea towel), and using a water spray, spray the cloth until damp. Leave the cloth on top of the knitted piece and allow it to dry completely. As each yarn is different, refer to the ball band and press the pieces according to the instructions given. Blocking the knitted fabric will help the pieces maintain their shape and give a smooth finish.

SEWING IN ENDS— Once you have pressed your finished pieces, sew in all loose ends. Thread a darning needle with yarn, weave needle along approximately 5 sts on wrong side of fabric, and pull thread through. Weave needle in opposite direction approximately 5 sts, pull thread through, and cut end of yarn.

MATTRESS STITCH—This method of sewing-up is worked on the right side of the fabric and is ideal for matching stripes. Mattress stitch should be worked one stitch in from the edge of the work to give the best finish. With RS of work facing, lay the two pieces to be joined edge to edge. Insert needle from WS between edge st and second st. Take yarn to opposite piece, insert needle from front, pass the needle under two rows, bring it back through to the front and insert it again into the opposite piece at the point of its last exit.

BACK STITCH—Pin the pieces with right sides together. Insert needle into fabric at end, one stitch or row from edge, and take the needle around the two edges to secure them. Insert needle into fabric just behind where last stitch came out and make a short stitch. Re-insert needle where previous stitch started, and bring up needle to make a longer stitch. Re-insert needle where last stitch ended. Repeat to end, taking care to match any pattern features.

Yarn Information

You can purchase yarns two ways, from the yarn shop where you will find really helpful, knowledgeable staff and an amazing array of products, knitting yarns, needles, buttons, and beads, or from the Internet, where there are many really good yarn websites—you can find them easily when you put in a search for knitting yarns. These sites often show the whole spectrum of colors in yarn ranges, have lots of information available, and are a fantastic resource. However, before you begin knitting, visit a yarn store so you can get an idea of what is available, as nothing compares with the tactile quality of touching and feeling a ball of yarn. When you visit the yarn shop you will find an amazing array of colors and textures. The choice is unbelievable, and you will feel like a kid in a candy shop. Choosing which yarn to use can be quite daunting; in the knitting patterns here I have specified the yarn used because it is often the texture and colors that inspire the design. In this book I have used a variety of different yarn types, some for practical reasons, some because of the color, texture, shine and quality. Below I have listed some of the yarns I have chosen along with their unique qualities and notes on availability.

Animal fiber yarns

Wool

Wool is the traditional yarn that we knit with and comes from the fleece of sheep. Wool is very warm to wear, as it holds in the heat, and is great for accessories. Traditionally wool can be itchy and scratchy, and when you wear it close to the skin—a hat, scarf or gloves—it can be quite uncomfortable. Many yarn spinners now make very soft wool blends using different types of fleece. I suggest you look for yarns made of merino wool blends, as these are the softest. Wool yarns can look different, depending on how they are spun. Woolen spun, which produces tweed yarns, is dyed before spinning, the color and texture added as the yarn is spun. Worsted spun is spun first and then dyed afterwards, producing a soft, continuous yarn that usually comes in many beautiful colors. This spinning process also works with synthetic yarn and yarn that is specially treated to make it machine washable. Look on the label for washing instructions.

If you use a traditional wool yarn that is slightly coarse in texture, I suggest that after you have knitted it, hand wash it with some fabric softener. This will make the fabric feel wonderfully soft.

Cashmere

Cashmere is a luxury fiber, and pure cashmere yarns can be expensive. Because of this reality, many spinners combine it with wool to make it more affordable. These yarns feel wonderful to knit with, touch and wear.

Silk

Silk is a wonderful fiber and absorbs color when it is dyed to produce beautiful, vivid shades, however it is expensive to produce and thus is often mixed with other yarn fibers.

Mohair

Mohair comes from the Angora goat, and when spun, produces a light, fluffy, and very warm yarn. Because it is hairy you can knit this yarn to the same gauge as a thicker yarn using bigger needles, and the hairy fibers give the fabric stability.

Angora

Angora comes from the Angora rabbit. The luxurious silky hairs are very short and difficult to spin without combining it with wool or synthetic fibers. As it is expensive to produce it is ideal for small projects. Do take care, as the short hairs in this yarn tend to shed and can cause an allergic reaction.

Vegetable fiber yarns

Cotton

Cotton yarns are now very popular and made from the cotton plant. The yarn is soft and non-itchy, which is good for sensitive skin, but it does not have much elasticity. I love the way cotton yarns when knitted enhance the texture of cables and stitch structures. When knitted it can be quite heavy, so it's ideal for small projects like purses. It is extremely important that, when knitting cotton, the correct gauge is obtained, otherwise the project will not wear well.

Linen

Linen yarn is obtained from the flax plant. It is strong and extremely durable, but if knitted as a solid fiber it can be tough and resemble rope. This yarn is most often blended with other fibers to make it softer and less difficult to work with.

Synthetic yarns

Nylon, acrylic and viscose yarns are widely available in the marketplace. Made from man-made fibers, they come in many varieties, and you can find exciting, experimental yarns in wonderful colors. I especially love the metallic yarns that add sparkle and glamour to many fashions. These yarns are great, but there's a caveat: They will not have the long-lasting properties of natural yarns.

INTERCHANGEABLE YARN TABLE

I have designed and photographed the projects in this book using specific yarns as detailed. Since the patterns were first published some yarns and shades have become discontinued and availability may be limited.If you are unable to locate the exact yarn detailed you will need to substitute the yarn. Below is a table of yarns from my yarn range that are interchangeable. The yarns are listed by the generic weight as given at the beginning of each pattern alongside of the yarns from my ranges which are interchangeable.

GENERIC WEIGHT	LOUISA HARDING YARN
Double knitting-weight yarn 4 mm (US 6) needles Average tension 22 sts x 30 rows	Impression, Kashmir DK, Mulberry, Jasmine, Kimono Angora, Kimono Angora Pure, Merletto, Grace & Grace Hand Dyed
Worsted-weight yarn 4.5 mm (US 7) needles Average tension 20 sts x 26/28 rows	Glisten, Albero, Nautical Cotton, Cinnabar, Grace & Grace Hand Dyed
Aran-weight yarn 5 mm (US 8) needles Average tension 18 sts x 24 rows	Kashmir Aran, Kimono Ribbon, Kimono Ribbon Pure
Bulky-weight yarn 7/8 mm (US 10½/11) needles Average tension 13 sts x 16/17 rows	Ca'd'Oro, Sari Ribbon, Thalia

SUBSTITUTING YARNS

If you substitute a yarn not from the Louisa Harding range of yarns YOU MUST MATCH THE TENSION/GAUGE stated in the pattern, all the patterns in this book are worked out mathematically to the specified generic yarn weight, If the correct tension is not achieved your project will turn out too big or too small. The tension will be stated on the yarn label, and I strongly recommend that you knit a swatch of your chosen yarn before embarking on the design.Saying this, it can be fun to substitute yarns and starts you thinking creatively about knitting.

YARN DISTRIBUTORS

The following companies distribute Louisa Harding Yarns.
Their websites have helpful information regarding yarns, shade cards and yarn store locators.

USA: Web: www.euroyarns.com
Email: euroyarns@knittingfever.com
Tel: 800 645 3457
Fax: 631 598 5800

Canada: Web: www.diamondyarn.com
Email: diamond@diamondyarn.com
Tel: 416 736 6111

Europe: Web: www.designeryarns.uk.com
Email: alex@designeryarns.uk.com
Tel: +44 0 1535 664222
Fax: +44 0 1535 664333

CONTACT DETAILS
Email: enquires@louisaharding.co.uk

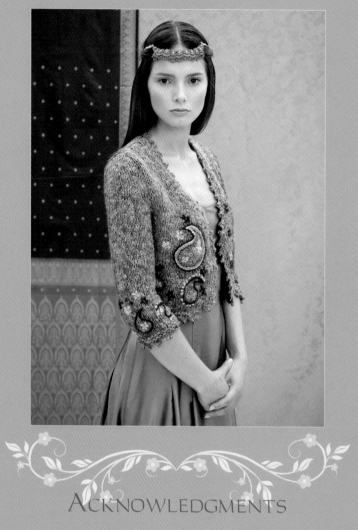

Acknowledgments

This book is dedicated to all the "cardigan girls" out there. To the sisterhood of that uniquely female creative gene, which we are unable to suppress. Thank you always for your encouragement and support.

As always, I thank Stephen Jessup for wonderful photographs and for being my rock. I also thank our children Belle & Oscar—thankfully, children change everything. My wonderful family is always an inspiration and are always on hand for support and guidance. I would also like to thank the whole team at Knitting Fever: Sion Elalouf, who believed in me and gave me the exciting opportunity of launching my own yarn line, and also Jay, Jeff, and Haydee, who are always there and happy to help.

This book would not be possible without the help of the following people:
My wonderful knitters, Betty Rothwell, Mrs. Marsh, Mary Butler, Mrs. Wilmot, Jay Ingram-Seal, Mary Potter and Daphne Harding. I would like to thank all the beautiful models: Laine Wilson, Cara Treweek, Kirsty Dunning, Caroline Senior, Hannah Whittaker, Jen Saul, Helen Stinton, Khiara Parker, Helen Preistly, Casandra Fletcher, Amelia Enright, Crystyn Williams, Janine McCauley and Catherine Hudson.

Thank you to Vicky Adamson, Michael Richmond and Claire Salter for being such wonderfully creative make-up and hair artists, and to Andy Richards, Laura Lamb and Guy Bishop for being such able and accommodating assistants. For great pattern-checking support I would like to thank Stella Smith and Tricia McKenzie.

Finally, thank you to Trisha Malcom, Wendy Williams and the fantastic team of women at Sixth&Spring Books for their support, understanding and encouragement in the exciting realization and transformation of an idea to a beautiful book.